AM I REALLY SAVED?

Reasonable answers to common questions and doubts about Biblical salvation

This book is the perfect companion for those who:

- ❖ Have struggled with doubts about their faith
- ❖ Have recently made a decision to follow Christ
- ❖ Are counseling others in their faith
- ❖ Are in home study groups

By
KEVIN MCCARTHY

Am I Really Saved?

Reasonable answers to common questions and doubts about Biblical salvation

Kevin McCarthy

Copyright © 2014 Kevin McCarthy

Published by Inpower Books,
A division of Inpower Solutions Group, Inc.

Visit our blog at: www.ThinkLikeJesus.Org

Cover design by Chris McCarthy
Editing & typeset by Chrissy Conklin

ISBN: 0615964869
ISBN-13: 978-0615964867 (Inpower Books)

For bulk copies of this book, Contact:
Inpower Books toll free at 877-527-9613

DEDICATION

This book is dedicated to every person who has struggled with this subject and battled to keep the faith. Whether you feel victorious or defeated by this battle of the mind, I pray this book satisfies your mind, speaks to your soul and provides the assurance you seek.

I also dedicate this book to my wife, Rachel, son Christopher and daughter Noelle, who witnessed and endured all of my own battles and struggles with this same question. They are my heroes.

For all the pastors and leaders who help shepherd the rest of the body of Christ, thank you for your continued service! Be strong and of good courage.

ACKNOWLEDGMENTS

I thank Rachel for her endurance and perseverance as she spent many lonely days and nights during my journey studying this subject and writing this book.

Special thanks for my son, Chris, for creating the front/back cover for the book and to Noelle and her friends for helping pick the final colors.

Thank you to Chrissy Conklin for your hard work of re-typing and editing the manuscript.

Thank you Garry Senna, my first pastor and life-long friend, for laying a firm Biblical foundation in me through mentorship, for baptizing me in an ice cold Jacuzzi and for marrying Rachel and me over 27 years ago. The journey continues, my friend.

TABLE OF CONTENTS

Preface

Years ago I found myself in a very dark place that caused me to deeply question everything I thought I believed. Even twenty years after making a decision to follow Jesus, leading worship bands, preaching from pulpits, sharing Christ on the street corners and becoming an ordained minister, I found myself in a painful, lonely place questioning my salvation – even the very existence of God and validity of Christ. Maybe you can relate?

As I began my journey of spiritual recovery, I knew I needed to start with the very basics. I needed to understand if, in fact, there really was a Creator, and, if the Creator really had a Son, Jesus Christ. I spent countless hours in a library studying not just Christian works, but also that of other religions. I even thoroughly read books by famous atheists wondering if their arguments were sound. After extensively reasoning through the logical arguments and evaluating the historical evidence, I ultimately came to the conclusion that Christ is exactly who he claimed himself and hundreds of eyewitnesses claimed him to be. This was just the foundation. I still needed to know if I really was saved.

In 1984 I came to believe Christ was the Son of God purely based on an emotional, blind-faith decision to follow Him after hearing and reading some of the Bible. Today I have reconfirmed that belief through research and reasoning. Faith and reasoning are not mutually exclusive. Rather, they are complimentary to a strong faith.

Once I was reasonably satisfied with the authenticity and historicity of Jesus Christ, I then questioned my own salvation and my relationship to Him. It seemed a reasonable quest to make sure I was not just saying I was a Christian. I needed to know if I truly became a Christian in 1984 or was I just deluded and living a lie. If I truly did become a Christian, was it possible that I was no longer a Christian; that I had lost my salvation?

The work contained in these pages represents over 1000 hours of research coupled with much prayer and soul searching.

Though it is impossible to completely lay aside all presuppositions or biases, I did my best. I was willing to accept whatever truth could be discovered regardless of whether or not it would shatter my faith and turn my world upside-down. In essence, I was hungry for truth and tired of believing what others had told me; I needed to know first-hand.

I did not do this research with the intention of writing a book. But, I did document all of my research and findings. It was at the conclusion of my research when my questions were satisfied that I decided to compile my research into a thesis with the hopes it would benefit others.

Now I am asking you to do what I set out to not do – that is, to believe what someone else is teaching rather than learning it yourself.

With that in mind, I decided to do a few things to help you come to your own conclusions without having to spend the same countless hours of research.

First, I decided to write a concise book with my findings. Next, I decided to format the book into two sections. Section one is my summary and will serve to give you a broad understanding of salvation and the reasonable questions many of us ask at one time or another.

The second section is a verse-by-verse exegesis of scripture. That is, I endeavored to interpret from scripture what is actually meant rather than reading into it what is not there (eisegesis). To do this, I studied biblical hermeneutics to help me in my quest to rightly divide the Word of God.

I better understand how to read scripture while keeping in mind the context, such as: Who wrote the verse? To whom did he write it? What was going on in the culture? What prompted the writing? What was the author trying to convey or address? What would the early readers have understood?

I better understood literary genres and devices such as parallelisms, similes, hyperboles, anthropomorphisms and the like.

Learning how to exegetically interpret scripture opened my eyes to how often I had previously interpreted a scripture to mean something it was never meant to say.

Section two represents all of my scriptural research and the thought processes that went into each verse. I took each verse and studied it in context using biblical encyclopedias for historical context and Greek references to better understand verb tenses. The goal of section two is to provide you with a detailed understanding of each verse related to or thought to be related to salvation.

I encourage you to take the time to do your own in-depth study of soteriology (the study of the religious doctrine of salvation). Use this book as a starting place. Then, use the accompanying workbook (expected Fall 2014) for your personal use or in small group studies to further reason through the scriptures.

My prayer is this study encourages you as it did me.

If you would like to be notified when the workbook is available or if you would like to comment on the study, visit www.ThinkLikeJesus.Org

INTRODUCTION

According to Gallup, "eight in ten Americans consider themselves to be Christians[1]". The Pentecostal Evangel reports, "84% of Americans claim to be Christian[2]". Yet, when survey questions narrow in scope to reflect the actual lifestyle of the respondents, only seven percent[3] appear to be living a lifestyle commensurate with what the Bible describes as a disciple or follower of Jesus Christ – what we will refer to as a genuine believer, a truly born-again Christian. If only seven percent are living their faith, what happened to the rest?

This is where you and I come in – the rest. If you consider yourself a Christian, but believe that you do not necessarily live up to the high standards you believe you should, then you have probably asked yourself, or, you may now be asking the same question I have asked: Am I really saved?

This is a question common to most Christian people. It is an honest question which deserves an honest, well-researched answer.

Based on the survey results above, I believe it might be safe to assume there is a large group of people that *believe* they are "Christians" but may not have had a genuine, born-again conversion as described in Scripture.

Another possibility is that there are a lot of people who call themselves Christians who, in fact, are Christians but have personal, life struggles which might cause others, and, even themselves to question their Christianity.

It is also possible that if, according to George Barna, there is such as wide gap between those who claim to be Christians and those who demonstrate the "Christian" lifestyle, then a large percentage of those claiming to be Christians might, indeed, be living in what has often been referred to as a backslidden condition[4].

Whichever the case, wherever you find yourself, answering the question, "Am I really saved?" is an important one, not only for eternity, but, also for the empowerment to work through our struggles and to live a more exemplary Christian life.

So then, this brings us to the heart of our discussion:

What does it mean to be a genuine believer?

Can a genuine believer backslide to the point of losing his or her salvation?

The answers to these questions contained within these pages will change your life.

How to read this book

Section one (pages 13 through 30) lays out what is means to be a Christian based on Scripture.

Section two (pages 31 through 56) provides answers to the most common questions about whether or not we can lose our salvation.

Reading the sections one and two may be enough to resolve all your doubts.

The Appendix (the remaining 93 pages of the book) provides the scriptural research that went into determining the answers provided in the first sections. I would encourage you to study each scripture for yourself in context. However, the Appendix is provided as a resource and is not necessarily meant to be read like the first part of the book.

SECTION ONE: Foundations of Faith

CHAPTER ONE

Who Do You Say That I Am?

Before one is truly ready to receive the full impact of the Gospel of Jesus Christ, one must have an understanding of God's holiness, humankind's sinfulness, humanity's separation from God, and Christ's work of redemption. If we do not understand these basic conditions, the soil of our heart will not be fertile enough to produce eternal fruit when the seed of God's word is sown. This is why Jesus uses a parable of the four seeds as described in the Gospel of Matthew. (See Matthew 13)

"But who do you say that I am" Matthew 16:15

Finally, we must also understand the biblical answers to two very important questions presented in Scripture. One is where Jesus asked His disciples, "But who do you say that I am" (Matt 16:15)? The other is where the Roman jailer said to Paul and Silas, "Sirs, what must I do to be saved" (Acts 16:30)? Answering these questions may seem simple. In fact, the common answers may be "the Son of God" and "believe in Jesus", respectively. Nevertheless, if that is the depth of our understanding of our Savior and His gift of salvation, then it is probably also the depth of our relationship to Him – if we have one at all.

We ask: is Jesus merely a created Son of God? Is He simply an enlightened man? Is He more than a man but not God Himself? Could

He be one hundred percent man and one hundred percent God?

Believing in the correct Jesus Christ is essential to our eternal destiny. In other words, placing our trust in the *real* Jesus versus a distorted Jesus means the difference between life and death.

We must also define some of the terminology used in American Christian culture such as "believe". We will learn that saying we believe is only as good as our life demonstrates that belief. Most people in America say they believe, but the surveys show otherwise.

The Real Jesus

Having a correct understanding of Jesus Christ, the Son of God (and God, the Son) was important to Jesus. He asked His disciples, "But who do you say I am?" to which Peter replied, "You are the Christ, the Son of the living God." Jesus said to him, "blessed are you, Simon Barjona, because flesh and blood did not reveal this to you, but My Father who is in heaven" (Matt 16:15-17).

Even Paul reasoned from the Scripture [the Old Testament at the time] to explain who Jesus is to anyone who would listen (Acts 17:2-3). The Jesus that saves us, the Jesus who we serve, must be the Jesus of Scripture – no more, no less. If we do not put our trust in the correct Jesus – the Jesus of the Bible – then, our faith is in vain (1 Cor 15:2). Who do you say that He is?

If we do not put our trust in the correct Jesus – the Jesus of the Bible – then, our faith is in vain.

In God's great plan of redemption, He sent His son, Jesus Christ, to be the ultimate and final sacrifice for our sins. Who is this Son of God? Is He a man elevated to some level of deity? Is He a prophet simply proclaiming God's message? Or, is He God, who clothed himself in the form of man (Phil 2:6-7) in order to shed His unblemished blood for our sins?

Any serious Bible student who approaches the word of God with intellectual integrity (that is, honestly searching for the truth, not just trying to defend a presupposed position), will readily discover that Jesus Christ is, in fact, God in human form. All we have to do is review some key points to resolve this issue plainly through Scripture.

If you feel that scripture alone is insufficient to establish the authenticity of Christ, I refer you to a couple great works on the matter that provide more evidence outside of scripture: Evidence That Demands a Verdict by Josh McDowell and The Case for Christ by Lee Strobel (as well as the other Case For books in the series).

Who created the world?

Genesis tells us "in the beginning *God* created the heavens and the earth" (Gen 1:1). Yet, John's gospel proclaims, "all things came into being by *Him* [Jesus]" (John 1:3)

Who raised Jesus from the dead?

Naturally speaking, a dead man cannot raise himself up. Yet, Jesus said, "*I* lay down my life that *I* may take it up again" (John 10:18) and He said, "Destroy this temple, and in three days *I* will raise it up. But He was speaking of the temple of His body" (John 2:19, 21). Jesus says *He* will raise himself up.

However, Luke reports, "This Jesus *God* raised up again" (Acts 2:32) and, "The *God* of our Fathers raised up Jesus" (Acts 5:30). Furthermore, "*God* raised Him [Jesus] up on the third day" (Acts 10:40). Who raised Him up, Jesus or God?

Who is allowed to receive worship?

God, and God alone, is to be worshipped. Exodus 34:14 makes it clear that "you shall not worship any other god". Yet, the magi came to worship Jesus (Matt 2:2) and Jesus never refused worship from any of His followers (Matt 14:33, 28:9, 28:17; John 9:38).

Who can forgive sins but God?

The scriptural case for Jesus being God is overwhelming and we have only scratched the surface. The final point on His deity that we will make here is to point out the most significant issues that the Jewish leaders had with Jesus. Namely, He was claiming to be God and demonstrating that claim by forgiving sins to which "the Scribes and the Pharisees began to reason, saying, 'who is this man who speaks blasphemies? Who can forgive sins, but God alone?'" (Luke 5:21). Do you believe Jesus is the Son of God and God, the Son?

Four foundational truths

God is holy

This may seem elementary, but God *is* holy. This means that every aspect of Him is pure and righteous. He cannot sin. He cannot lie. He did not create sin nor can He have an intimate relationship with any creature that is sinful by nature – human beings. Isaiah 6:3 speaks of the angels declaring, "Holy, holy, holy, is the Lord of Hosts, the whole earth is full of your glory". In addition, Revelation echoes the chant, "For you alone are holy; for all the nations will come and worship before you, for your righteous acts have been revealed" (Rev 15:4).

Humankind is sinful

Humankind is alienated from its creator because of our sinful condition. That is, because we are sinners and God is holy, we are separated from him. Humankind took on this sin "nature" when Adam chose to disobey his maker in the Garden of Eden. Paul explains it this way, "therefore, just as through one man sin entered into the world, and death through sin, and so death spread to all men, because all sinned" (Rom 5:12). As a result, "for all have sinned and fall short of the glory of God" (Rom 3:23).

However, even if the first sin of Adam did not make us sinners in God's sight, any one of our sins would be sufficient to keep us from a right relationship with God. It is no wonder that all men walked away from the harlot when Jesus said, "He who is without sin among you, let him be the first to throw a stone" (John 8:7).

Humanity is separated from God

No matter how hard we try, we will never be sinless. We can never be good enough for a perfect, pure, holy God. Our sins have separated us from God (Isa 59:2). Nowhere does the Bible describe God using a scale with our sins on one side and our good works on the other. One little white lie is sinful enough to keep us eternally separated from God –only Christ can rectify this separation.

Because of God's holiness, righteousness and justice, any sin, no matter how trivial, must be judged and the penalty paid by the sinner. Death – eternal separation from God – is the penalty: "For the wages of sin is death" (Rom 6:23).

Jesus Christ reconciles humanity to God

The Good News (the Gospel) is that Jesus Christ paid the penalty for our sins. From the beginning of time, God knew that humans would be separated from Him and would require a solution to bring humanity back into right relationship with Him (Acts 2:23). Therefore, in His foreknowledge, He prepared the ultimate sacrifice that would act as a buffer, a mediator, between God and humanity – Jesus Christ (1 Tim 2:5). Paul writes, "even so through the obedience of the One [Jesus Christ] the many will be made righteous" (Rom 5:19).

When we finally grasp the reality of the above points, we should feel the heavy weight of our hopelessness apart from Christ. It is only in this place of utter despair and hopelessness that we are ready to truly receive and appreciate the gospel message. Until we are in a place where we are at the end of our rope, as the saying goes, will we be ready to surrender ourselves to Christ. Until we can do so, we are not ready to receive His salvation. He did not come to save the healthy, He came to save the sick; He came to save the lost.

Conclusion

Jesus Christ is our only answer to the problem of sin. Since humanity is separated from God because of its sinful nature, only a perfectly sinless sacrifice would reconcile us back to a holy God.

Jesus became this perfect, sinless sacrifice and died on our behalf. He was the only one who could have paid this ultimate price for us. No one else can save us. We certainly cannot save ourselves.

There is a reason Jesus asked "who do you say that I am?" There are many false Christs (anti-Christs). We need to identify and follow the true, resurrected Jesus, otherwise our faith is in vain.

CHAPTER TWO

What Must I do to be Saved?

Salvation – the free gift of God (Rom 6:23) whereby humans are restored to a right and personal relationship with the living, holy God – comes as a result of hearing the true gospel and then, by God's grace, responding through faith to His call to surrender. In order to respond, the Holy Spirit must bring to the hearer a conviction of sin and a heart of repentance (repentance: the ability and desire to turn from sin to God; to change one's way of thinking to line up with God's way of thinking).

"Sirs, what must I do to be saved" (Acts 16:30)

Recognize our Hopelessness

This conviction is not a worldly sorrow as if one was just caught with one's hand in the cookie jar. It is a heart-felt, deep-seated anguish over the realization that we are separated from God because of our sins. No matter how small, our sins are an offense to a holy God. We accept that "all of us have become like one who is unclean, and all our righteous deeds are like a filthy garment" (Isa 64:6).

Jesus describes how we should feel in His parable of the Pharisee and the tax collector:

> "Two men went up into the temple to pray, one was a Pharisee [a very pious, religious person] and the other a tax collector. The Pharisee stood and was praying this to himself: 'God, I thank you that I am not like other

people: swindlers, unjust, adulterers, or even like this tax collector. I fast twice a week; I pay tithes of all that I get.' But the tax collector, standing some distance away, was even unwilling to lift up his eyes to heaven, but was beating his breast, saying, 'God be merciful to me, a sinner!'

I tell you, this man went to his house justified rather than the other; for everyone who exalts himself will be humbled, but he who humbles himself will be exalted" (Luke 18:10-14).

We deceive ourselves when we believe we can approach God any other way than the tax collector. We would do good to remember the words of Jeremiah: "The heart is more deceitful than all else and is desperately sick; who can understand it?" (Jer 17:9) Do you fully recognize your hopelessness without Christ? Do you grieve over sin?

Counting the Costs

If salvation is a gift, how can there be any costs involved? It is true that salvation is a *free* gift that comes to us by the grace of God through faith. However, accepting this gift will cost us our very lives! Not necessarily our physical lives, as in being a martyr for Christ. When Jesus refers to our "lives", He is referring to everything we hold dear and esteem higher than we esteem Him.

Paul writes, "and He [Jesus] died for all, so that they who live might no longer live for themselves, but for Him who died and rose again on their behalf (2 Cor 5:15). When we make a decision to accept the gift of salvation offered by God through Jesus, we must understand and accept the fact that our lives will no longer belong to us to live for our own passions and desires. We must be willing to surrender those passions and desires to the will of God for our lives. We must live for His passions and desires.

Jesus puts it bluntly: "If anyone wishes to come after Me, he must deny himself, and take up his cross and follow Me. For whoever wishes to save his life will lose it; but whoever loses his life for My sake will find it. For what will it profit a man if he gains the whole world and forfeits his soul? Or what will a man give in exchange for his soul?" (Matt 16:24-26).

The Greek word for "lives" here is not *pneuma* referring to our natural or physical lives. It is *psyche* referring to the essence of who we are; all that we hold dear, everything we believe about ourselves that makes us who we are. Therefore, to come to Jesus, we must be willing to surrender all of our passions, desires and identity and place the entirety of our trust in Him.

For instance, Jesus explains that to come to Him we must love Him more than we love our parents, children, spouse or even our own lives (Matt 10:37-39). Luke elaborates on the significance of counting the costs:

> "If anyone comes to me [Jesus], and does not *hate* his own father and mother and wife and children and brothers and sisters, yes, even his own life, he cannot be My disciple". He does not mean literally to *hate* them. He means that when it comes to our love and commitment to Christ, our relationship with our natural family should pale in comparison. Luke goes on to say, "For which of you, when he wants to build a tower, does not first sit down and calculate the cost to see if he has enough to complete it? … Or, what king, when he sets out to meet another king in battle, will not first sit down and consider whether he is strong enough with ten thousand men to encounter the one coming against him with twenty thousand?" (Luke 14:26-33).

Repent and Be Converted!

Once confronted with the truth of the gospel with ready hearts (fertile soil – Matthew 13:23), we must then repent of our sins. This is more than simply asking God to forgive us. The Greek word for repentance, *metanoia*, literally means to change our thinking, to turn *from* sin and *toward* God. Repentance says to God, "I am deeply sorry for my sins and I make a commitment to change the way I am living for myself and will start living for you. I will turn away from (albeit, by God's grace empowering us to do so) all that is sin and live for you!"

How important is this? Jesus said, "I tell you, no, but unless you repent, you will all likewise perish" (Luke 13:3). Peter preached it at Pentecost: "Therefore repent and return, so that your sins may be wiped away" (Acts 3:19).

The message of the gospel as taught by Christ and His apostles is, "repent and turn to God, performing deeds appropriate to repentance" (Acts 26:20).

Paul's words to the people of Athens seem just as appropriate for us today as we have demonstrated our own ignorance: "Therefore having overlooked the times of ignorance, God is now declaring to men that all people everywhere should repent" (Acts 17:30).

With Your Mouth Confess

When we are truly ready to repent, we must then confess Christ. That is, we must declare publicly and aloud who Christ is and who we have now become in Him – a born-again, genuine believer. (As a side note, we use the term genuine believer in place of "Christian" because the latter term is so watered-down; it has lost its original meaning).

Paul teaches us, "that if you confess with your mouth Jesus as Lord, and believe in your heart that God raised Him from the dead, you will be saved; for with the heart a person believes, resulting in righteousness, and with the mouth he confesses, resulting in salvation" (Rom 10:9-10). Notice we confess Jesus as Lord – not just Savior. Moreover, this confession is with the mouth, aloud, in other words. There are no secret genuine believers. Jesus makes that clear when He states, "Therefore everyone who confesses Me before men, I will also confess him before My Father who is in heaven. But whoever denies Me before men, I will also deny him before My Father who is in heaven" (Matt 10:32-33).

The first thing one must do upon being born-again is to tell family and friends. Make a declaration of your new relationship with Christ. This may cause some anxiety by not knowing how they will react. Nevertheless, if our encounter with Christ was genuine, we will not be ashamed of the Gospel (Rom 1:16). Are you embarrassed to make a stand for Christ?

What it means to "believe"

The phrase," I believe in Jesus", may be the cornerstone of the problem in American Christianity. We have so watered down the concept of "believing" that we are way off the mark of how the Bible defines believing in Jesus.

True, we must *believe* in order to be saved (Rom 10:9-10). The Apostles preached, "Believe in the Lord Jesus, and you will be saved, you and your household" (Acts 16:31). Of course, the most popular of New Testament verses used for believing: "For God so loved the world that he gave His only begotten Son, that whoever believers in Him shall not perish, but have everlasting life" (John 3:16).

"You believe that God is one, you do well; the demons also believe, and shudder" (James 2:19)

However, this believing by definition is more than saying *I believe*. It is more than accepting historical facts and determining that Jesus must be real, therefore, *I believe* in Him. It is more than attending your childhood "Christian" church and saying *I believe*; or, having been baptized as a child so therefore you *believe*. James points out that, "you believe that God is one, you do well; the demons also believe, and shudder" (James 2:19). Anyone can say *I believe*. The demons believe – they know that Christ is God. Yet, we know instinctively that demons cannot be saved.

Believing in a biblical context describes an outward action. When one truly believes in the risen Lord, one's life radically begins to change and that belief is demonstrated by "performing deeds appropriate to repentance" (Acts 26:20). A genuine believer accepts God's word for what it is, not the word of men, but the word of God (1 Thes 2:13). A genuine believer desires to obey all that Christ teaches (Matt 29:19). This is not to say that a genuine believer will not sin. Rather, his or her life will be characterized by a genuine submission to Christ with a heart attitude of repentance when sins are committed. Their life will not be characterized by a life of darkness (John 8:12)

Jesus sums it up best, "why do you call Me, Lord, Lord, and do not do what I say? Everyone who comes to Me and hears My word and acts on them, I will show you whom he is like: he is like a man building a house, who dug deep and laid a foundation on the rock; and when a flood occurred, the torrent burst against that house and could not shake it, because it had been well built. But the one who has heard and has not acted accordingly, is like a man who built a house on the ground without any foundation; and the torrent burst against it and immediately it collapsed, and the ruin of that house was great" (Luke 6:46-49), emphasis added). Do you really believe?

Conclusion

The answer to what we must do to be saved creates a paradox. On the one hand, it is a simple message: Believe in Jesus Christ. On the other hand, it is more difficult: we must die to ourselves.

Depending on how the Gospel is presented, it might seem easy to make a decision to follow Christ. And, a decision is certainly where it starts.

One might visit a church, listen to a sermon that has little to do with salvation, and, then raise one's hand while everyone has their heads bowed during what is generally referred to as an altar call. Does that person get saved because of a simple prayer? It is definitely possible, maybe even probable.

These types of altar calls, though effective for salvation, may, however, be setting wrong expectations about what it means to be a Christian and to have a relationship with Christ.

If we pray a "sinner's prayer" at a random altar call and leave expecting that we are suddenly changed, that we are going to experience some amazing differences in the way we act and feel, without a clear understanding of what it means to be saved, we could get disillusioned and disenchanted. This could be a big reason so many people wrestle with doubts about their salvation.

Have you ever thought or heard someone say "I tried that but it didn't work". It is as if saying a simple prayer was meant to free someone from an addiction or something else miraculous.

Some people do, in fact, experience a radical conversion like Paul on the road to Damascus and are able to pinpoint the very moment of their salvation. They have an experience that is a life-changing event. They do get miraculously set free from an addiction or bad habit. But, this is not often the case.

Others are not exactly sure when they were saved. They just know that they are and they are certain about it. Maybe they just started going to church out of obligation to the friend that keeps inviting them. Or, the couple decided it would be good to raise their children with religion. But, somewhere along the way the Gospel changed them. Somewhere along the journey they came to a saving faith in Christ. Now they consider themselves a follower of Christ.

Regardless of when and how one became a Christian, the vast majority of Christians may have doubts from time to time. Some struggle with doubts more than others.

Having doubts about our salvation occasionally is normal. If our biblical knowledge is not strong, we may experience more frequent doubting. But, even if one has a strong scriptural knowledge and understanding, and never seems to have any doubts, a single life-altering event can shake even the firmest of foundations.

"Quick alter calls without good follow up may set wrong expectations about following Christ."

The next chapter helps us to better understand how to do a self-assessment to make sure we are in the faith.

Then, in Section Two, you will have the answers to a lot of the common questions asked by a majority of Christians at one time or another. We do not have to have a blind faith. We are not told to shut off our brains to have faith. Faith can be supported by reason. Section Two provides a basis for what has been referred to as a reasonable faith.

You're not alone in your quest for truth. Don't give up!

CHAPTER THREE

Can I Really Be Certain That I Am Saved?

If we are genuine believers, our belief (or faith) will be evident in a new nature. The fruit of our life will prove that we are saved.

The New Nature

"Therefore if anyone is in Christ, he is a new creature; the old things passed away; behold, new things have come" (2 Cor 5:17).

When we become a genuine believer, we are set free from the bondage of sin; we become slaves of righteousness (Rom 6:18). We no longer have to be slaves to our sinful passions and desires (Rom 6:6). The heavy burden of our sins no longer should weigh us down. Our sins no longer control or master us, we enter into the grace of God (Rom 6:14). We will "no longer live for the lusts of men, but for the will of God" (1Pet 4:2)

This is not to say that physiological addictions are not real, or, that they are suddenly and instantly abolished when we become a Christian. That belief would not hold up to reality. Sincere and godly Christians will often battle the same sins and addictions as those who do not believe in Christ. It is the human condition in a fallen world.

What is does mean is that when the decision to follow Christ is made, the Holy Spirit indwells us and gives us the power to say no to sin. Sometimes that power is felt immediately and realized and bondages are suddenly broken. Other times we might not recognize that power or be able to appropriate it because we are getting in our own way. We might need to be purposeful about changing the way we think. This might happen through prayer as we study the Word of God. Or, it might take the guidance of a professional counselor.

Whichever the case, our new nature is already given to us and Jesus stands ready to take on our burdens.

The Fruit of Conversion

We will begin to sense an internal change in our character. When the Spirit of the living God takes up residence in the heart of a genuine believer, the fruit of God's Spirit is, "love, joy, peace, patience, kindness, goodness, faithfulness, gentleness, self-control… those who belong to Christ have crucified the flesh with its passions and desires" (Gal 5:22, 24). Of course, this will always be a work-in-progress (called sanctification). However, we should notice a measure of change in these areas immediately with noticeable growth throughout our lives.

Peter exhorts us to grow in similar areas. He provides a list of areas in which we are to be diligent to grow. He says to our faith we are to add: moral excellence, knowledge, self-control, perseverance, godliness, brotherly kindness and love. If we are growing in these areas, we are both fruitful and useful to the Master (2 Pet 1:5-8).

If we are genuine believers, we will be devoted to our church (Acts 2:41), to the Scripture, to fellowship with our genuine believers, to sharing meals together, to prayer and to giving generously from our property and possessions to meet the needs around us (read Acts 2:42-49). Have you grown in these areas since you first believed?

With Birth Comes Growth – the Sanctification Process

When one truly believes, as we have defined from Scripture, one is truly born-again. Growth must follow the new birth. This growth is called the sanctification process; "without which no one will see the Lord" (Heb 12:14). This is a natural process for a new believer, although it is not an automatic process. We must be intentional about working with the Holy Spirit in our growth. The apostles are constantly exhorting us to "grow in the grace and knowledge of our Lord and Savior Jesus Christ" (2 Pet 3:18). We are to "be transformed be the renewing of [our] mind" (Rom 12:2). We are to be sanctified in the truth; "[God's] word *is* truth" (John 17:17, emphasis added); knowing that "this is the will of God, your sanctification" (1 Thes 4:3).

Sanctification means to be "set apart". We are to be recognized as children of God distinguishable from the world around us. We are to lay aside our old self – that part of us that looks to satisfy the lust of the eyes, lust of the flesh and pride of life (1 John 2:16) – and be renewed in the way we think (Eph 4:22-24). "Like newborn babies, long for the pure milk of the word, so that by it you may grow in respect to salvation" (1 Pet 2:2). Then we must leave "the elementary teaching about Christ" and "press on to maturity" (Heb 6:1).

If we say we believe but we are not being transformed into the image of Christ, we are deceiving ourselves. John provides assurance that "we have come to know Him, if we keep His commandments". If we do not, we are deceiving ourselves and the truth is not in us (1 John 2:3-4). This is not just keeping the *Ten Commandments*. This means we are obeying all the teachings of Christ and His apostles through Scripture (i.e., to grow!). If the Bible teaches we should faithfully attend church – we do it. If the Bible tells us that divorce is wrong (with few exceptions), then we strive to make our marriages work – no matter how many sacrifices are required of us. If the Bible teaches not to be drunk, then we stay sober. Obeying Jesus goes way beyond the Ten Commandments. It should be noted that we are not striving to keep a set of rules or laws that gain us favor with God for salvation. We obey Him because He has given us a new heart of love for Him. Do you love Him enough to obey His teachings? Do you obey Him because you love Him or only out of duty or obligation?

Conclusion

> *"If we are genuine believers, our belief (or faith) will be evident in a new nature."*

Now that we have studied what a genuine believer is according to biblical standards, we need to ask ourselves a sincere question: are we truly born-again? According to the Bible, do we have a personal, intimate relationship with the living God? Can we look at the fruit of our lives and recognize spiritual growth? Do we believe Jesus is God in the flesh? Do we accept that our works cannot add to what Christ has already accomplished on the cross – that is, to put us in right standing with him by grace through faith?

James says we do not want to be like the man who looks in the mirror but forgets what he sees as soon as he walks away (James 1:23-24). If the Holy Spirit shows you that your faith has never produced an internal heart change, then humble yourself right now and admit that to the Lord who loves you. You may recognize that you have never truly surrendered your will to His will. Yet, God has been drawing you and He is ready to receive you as one of His own. If now you have counted the costs of surrender and you are ready to give up your life *to* Him, then you will find new life *in* Him. The paradox is that salvation is free; yet it will cost you your life (that is your mind, will and emotions).

If you are ready to give Him your life, ask Him to forgive your sins (past, present and future). Believe by faith that your sins are forgiven. Let Him know you "repent" – that you will now commit to turn away from anything the Bible calls sin and will turn your life completely over to Christ today. Immediately, tell someone about your new commitment to Christ. Let people know that you are now a "born-again" Christian, a genuine believer and follower of Christ. Find a balanced, Bible-teaching church and get committed to its leadership. Ask them to help you grow in Christ.

Note: If you are not sure how to pray, then pray this prayer for salvation. Remember, this prayer alone is not a magic formula to get to heaven. Pray it only if you really mean it.

> *Lord Jesus, forgive my sins and have mercy on me – a sinner. I believe you are God who came in human form to save me. I understand I cannot do anything to earn my salvation. It comes by your grace as I put faith in you. Therefore, I declare that I believe Jesus Christ is my savior and Lord. I surrender my life and put my full trust in Jesus. I am ready to make a public declaration of my new faith in you for I am not ashamed to be called a child of God, a born-again believer. I repent of all of my sins and determine to serve you with my whole heart. I have counted the costs and I am willing to place you as the rightful Lord and authority over my life. I will love you more than I love my family and friends, or even myself.*
>
> *Thank you for accepting me as I am and for giving me a new heart, a brand new start at life regardless of my past and present failures. Thank you for forgiving all of my sins and for your grace to teach me to live a godly life, that glorifies you. I declare right now, [say this aloud], that Jesus Christ is Lord of all! I am now saved and set apart for His glory. Amen!*

If you made a decision to follow Jesus Christ, welcome to the family of God!

[This page intentionally left blank]

SECTION TWO:
Foundations for a reasonable faith

The next section will address some very common questions and concerns about our faith-commitment to Christ. How can I know for sure I am really saved? Why do I still sin? What if I backslide? Can I lose my salvation? These and many other questions that tend to haunt us after making a decision to surrender to Christ will be answered in this next section.

I should note that it is normal and perfectly acceptable to ask these questions regardless how long you have professed to be a Christian. We are never instructed to have a completely blind faith. It is okay to have what I like to refer to as a "reasonable" faith – a faith that can be strengthened through reasonable inquiry.

Works as Evidence of, not Conditions for My Salvation

"Even so, faith if it has no works, is dead, being by itself." (James 2:17)

Every genuine believer will produce good works because of his or her new nature. That is, they will show evidence in their lives that their conversion to Christ was real or genuine. As James said it so clearly, "even so faith, if it has no works, is dead, being by itself" (James 2:17). Jesus said, "Every good tree bears good fruit" (Matt 17:17) and we "will know them by their fruits" (Matt 17:20). However, as we discussed earlier, our good works do not result *in* our salvation. We are saved by grace through faith – this is the free gift of

God. We are not saved as a result of our works (Eph 2:8-9). Our works are the evidence of our faith (James 2:18).

So, if we cannot do any works to gain approval or favor with God and earn our salvation, then why would we think that once we are saved that our works are meritorious toward "keeping" our salvation? That would be like God saying, "You are not good enough for me, so I will save you by my grace through faith. Ah, but now that you are saved, I am keeping a scorecard. You better be good enough to continue to 'earn' my favor and stay saved." This is absurd! If you are truly saved, you will remain saved, as the rest of our discussions will demonstrate through Scripture.

Christ's Responsibility

Jesus will keep us; we will not perish.

We can never be good enough to earn God's favor. That is why we always have to rely on His grace to empower us to live a godly life (Titus 2:11-12). It is also why Christ takes the responsibility for our souls until the day we are home with Him. "My sheep hear My voice, and I know them, and they follow Me (following Him is the evidence, not the condition); and I give eternal life to them, and they will never perish; and no one will snatch them out of My hand. My Father, who has given them to Me, is greater than all; and no one is able to snatch them out of the Father's hand" (John 10:27-30). (See Appendix)

Paul encouraged the church in Philippi saying, "I am confident of this very thing, that He who began a good work in you will perfect it until the day of Christ Jesus" (Phil 1:6). Christ is the One who will perfect the work He began in you! "It is God who is at work in you, both to will and to work for *His* good pleasure" (Phil 2:13, emphasis added).

Jude also understood whose responsibility it is to keep us secure for eternity: "Now to Him who is able to keep you from stumbling and to *make* you stand in the presence of His glory blameless with great joy" (Jude 24, emphasis added). Christ makes us stand blameless in His presence.

Paul entrusted his soul to Christ and was convinced "that He is able to guard what I have entrusted to Him until that day" (2 Tim 1:12). And, Jesus sums it up best, "For this is the will of My Father, that everyone who beholds the Son and believes in Him will have eternal life, and I myself will raise him up on the last day" (John 6:40). Jesus takes full responsibility for those who are His. We can rest assured, if our conversion was genuine, no matter what we go through in life; He will hang on to us.

John Maxwell, author and speaker, shares a story that illustrates this point. This is a summary of the story:

A young boy was swimming in a lake when his father saw an alligator heading his way. The father yelled, catching the boys' attention. The boy quickly made his way back to the dock. Just as the father grabbed the boys' two arms, the alligator engulfed the boys' legs in its jaws. The father and the alligator pulled frantically, each one trying to seize control of the boy. A local farmer was driving by and heard the screaming. He came running with his gun and killed the alligator.

The boy survived with severe lacerations on his mauled legs from the alligators' teeth and deep wounds on his wrists from his father's grip. Later the boys' pastor came to visit him. The boy showed the pastor his battle wounds. The pastor commented on his legs to which the boy replied, "Oh, that's nothing. These are the wounds I am really proud of" as he showed his arms to the pastor. "These are where my father refused to let go of me," the boy said gleaming with confidence.

All genuine believers will go through many battles and we will receive many scars. However, like this boy's father, our heavenly Father will never let go. At times, it may feel like the enemy is going to destroy our lives. However, we can always have an internal peace knowing that our Father will never let go of our arms.

He Seals Our Eternity

We can know for certain that we have eternal life.

When we truly get born-again, the Holy Spirit of the living God comes to abide in our hearts. John says this is "how we know that we abide in Him and He in us, because He has given us of His Spirit" (1 John 4:13). Paul states, God "has sealed us and gave us His Spirit in our hearts as a pledge" (2 Cor 1:21-22). What is the seal of God? "Nevertheless, the firm foundation of God stands, having *this seal*, 'the Lord knows those who are His'" (2 Tim 2:19, emphasis added). We have a firm foundation that God knows His children. The Holy Spirit seals us for the day of redemption. (Eph 4:30)

Finally, John wrote in his epistles, "so that you may *know* that you *have* eternal life" (1 John 5:13, emphasis added). He did not write these things so we can *hope* we have eternal life. He says we can know for sure. Moreover, we know that we *now* have eternal life, not will have it in the future if we stay good. The eternity of a genuine believer is sealed!

If I am Really Saved, Why Do I Still Sin?

The Christian life is not a sinless life or one free from all addictions all the time.

This is a very fair question. Making a decision to follow Christ makes us righteous as far as God is concerned with regard to our position in his kingdom. It does not remove us from our humanity or the fallen world. After we receive salvation, we will participate in a sanctification process whereby the Holy Spirit works in us and through us to change our lives for God's glory. But, this is a process, not an instant result. And, we must cooperate with God's work in us even though we will continually be tempted by our own desires and the influences of others to sin. Let's take a closer look.

Conflict of Natures

Just because we become genuine believers does not mean that we will not sin. We do not become perfect while we live in this natural world. When Christ saves us, we become positionally perfect, that is, our spirits are reconciled to God. However, we are not practically perfect, that is, we will not live a perfect, sinless life in our natural bodies. Christ was the only sinless person to walk the earth since Adam before the fall.

Paul describes our renewed condition as a war between our flesh and our spirit (Gal 5:17). These two are in opposition to one another. "When Paul speaks about 'being in the flesh' throughout his writings, he is not talking about our physical nature as such, about physical passions and desires, but about a way of life, an orientation of life, a life lived apart from God's purposes for us[5]". As Christians, we will always have this constant tension between the flesh and the spirit.

Power of Sin Broken

The good news is that in Christ we are no longer in bondage to or slaves to sin. "Sin shall not be master over you" (Rom 6:14). We are "freed from sin and enslaved to God" (Rom 6:22). "And having been freed from sin, you have become slaves of righteousness" (Rom 6:18)

Paul explains that "though we walk in the flesh, we do not war according to the flesh, for the weapons of our warfare are not flesh, but divinely powerful for the destruction of fortresses" (2 Cor 10:3). We are no longer subject to the law of sin. We are under the grace of God, which helps us to say no to sin and live for righteousness (Titus 2:11-12).

We Have an Advocate

Finally, when we do succumb to temptations and sin, we can enjoy the peace of God knowing that "if anyone sins, we have an advocate with the Father, Jesus Christ the righteous" (1 John 2:1). Knowing this, "if we confess our sins, He is faithful and righteous to forgive us our sins and to cleanse us from all unrighteousness" (1 John 1:9)

The Christian life is not a sinless life or a life completely free from all addictions. However, when we sin, we can know that He stands immediately ready to forgive our sins upon our confession of them.

What If I Backslide?

We follow Christ, but the path is winding and the curves sometimes sharp.

First, let us define "backslide". The term itself only appears in the Old Testament and usually refers to the children of Israel in times where they rebel or turn away from God. In the New Testament context under the grace of God, this term can be defined as any measure of loss of commitment to or fervor for the Lord. This being the case, it is safe to say almost every genuine believer will backslide to one degree or another during his or her walk with the Lord. To use the title of a book, many of us take "Three Steps Forward, Two Steps Back" as we journey through life with Christ.

The cares of the world and deceitfulness of wealth (Matt 13:22) constantly challenge our walk. We have an active enemy who "comes only to steal and kill and destroy" (John 10:10); he is always trying to distract us from serving our God.

John warns that "even now many antichrists have appeared" (1 John 2:18) and thus exhorts us to "not love the world nor the things in the world… for all that is in the world, the lust of the flesh and the lust of the eyes and the boastful pride of life, is not from the Father" (1 John 2:15-16).

Our battle to stay faithful to Christ never ends. Our flesh constantly wars against our spirit. Look at Peter's life, for example. As an apostle, he walked side-by-side with the Lord and vowed that he would always be with him – even to death. Yet, three times Peter openly denied knowing Jesus. Can you imagine flat out denying Jesus? Peter cried like a baby at realizing what he had done. Later, Jesus not only forgave him and restored him, but also used Peter to be a powerful preacher (Acts 2:41). Thousands were saved under his ministry!

Today, some would say that if we deny Christ, we would lose our salvation. They say that we can backslide to the point of becoming "apostate" – and, they say, that no one who is apostate will go to heaven.

What If I become Apostate?

The term apostate is used much too loosely in modern Christianity.

Apostasy is another term we should define. The Greek word is *Apostasia* (Strong's #646) and is used only twice in the New Testament, Acts 21:21 and 2 Thes 2:3. Thayer's provides a short definition as "a falling away, defection, apostasy; in the Bible namely from true religion[6]". Spiros Zodhiates elaborates on the definition as: "In the majority of occasions, the verb is intransitive meaning that person does not depart from where he is, to go somewhere else, but strays away, having chosen from the beginning to stay away, not to believe instead of believing, in which case the verb *histemi* (Strong's #2476) is to be interpreted not as departing, but as standing away, placing oneself away; with the preposition *apo*, to stay away from[7]" (emphasis added).

In Acts 21:21, the word Apostasia is translated "forsake" (NASB) and refers to the Christian Jews staying away from the law of Moses; to not circumcise their children, and to not walk according to the customs.

In Two Thessalonians 2:3, the term is translated "apostasy". According to the definition from Zodhiates, this apostasy – a sign of the second coming – will be a group of people who "stand away from" something. This something is not defined in the same verse. In context, Paul describes this group in verses ten through twelve. These are people who "did not receive the love of the truth so as to be saved" (v. 11). He does this "in order that they all may be judged who did not believe the truth, but took pleasure in wickedness" (v. 12). (See notes in appendix for 2 Thessalonians 2:10-12, Page 85)

The term apostate is used much too loosely in modern Christianity. To say one is apostate is to say one has chosen not to believe the truth. It does not mean that a genuine believer can fall so far back from the Lord that they become apostate. It is impossible for a genuine believer to become apostate.

Paul dealt with a genuine believer who committed "immorality of such a kind as does not exist even among the Gentiles" (1 Cor 5:1). The man had committed adultery with his father's wife. Further, he appears to be arrogant and unrepentant. Therefore, Paul says, "I have decided to deliver such a one to Satan for the destruction of his flesh, that his spirit may be saved in the day of the Lord Jesus" (1 Cor 5:5). This story seems to indicate the man is a believer in a terribly backslidden state and will have to be removed from fellowship to reap the consequences of his actions – even if it kills his natural body. Paul seems to be confident that the man's salvation is not in question when he explains about the man, "that his spirit may be saved" (v. 5).

Knowing that none of us is immune from backsliding, we need to help one another. Paul writes, "We who are strong ought to bear the weakness of those without strength and not just please ourselves" (Rom 15:1). Further, "Brethren, even if anyone is caught in any trespass, you who are spiritual, restore such a one in a spirit of gentleness; each one looking to yourself, so that you too will not be tempted" (Gal 6:1).

What If I Stop Believing?

> *We take comfort in his promise to never leave us nor forsake us.*

We earlier discussed what it means to "believe". When we truly believe, that faith (or belief) will produce works. However, to say that if one stops believing, one loses salvation is a gross misunderstanding of Scripture.

It is not uncommon for genuine believers to entertain doubts. After all, the Christian faith is not meant to be a blind faith; it is a reasonable faith, a faith that can be reasoned through. However, what if those doubts take root and hinder me from believing that Christ is whom He says He is? What if I walk away from my faith? What if I get to the point that I simply quit believing and revert to my former life?

These are questions that continue to plague many people. However, if we recall our earlier points, if we are genuinely born-again, then Christ will not lose us. He promises He will never leave us. On the other hand, John says of those who are part of the congregation but then leave, "They went out from us, but they were not really of us; for if they had been of us, they would have remained with us" (1 John 2:19).

If we examine the fruit or proof of our conversion, and we know we are saved, then we should always remember Christ will not lose us. Though we stumble, we will not fall. It is said that we may fall on-board, but we can never fall overboard. Remember, Jesus says, "Truly, truly, I say to you, he who hears My word, and believes Him who sent Me, *has* [now has] eternal life, and does not come into judgment, but *has* passed [not will pass, but already has passed] out of death into life" (John 5:24, emphasis added).

What If I Choose To Live a Sinful Lifestyle?

When we choose to sin, our hearts will be troubled.

Paul summed up this question to the church in Rome: "How shall we who died to sin still live in it" (Rom 6:2)? Scripture gives us some strong evidence as to what a genuine believers' life looks like compared to a non-believer. The church in Corinth was being tolerant of *so-called* believers living in sin. Paul had to remind them to whom they belonged (1 Cor 6:19-20). In his second epistle to them, he challenged them to "test yourselves to see if you are in the faith; examine yourselves! Or, do you not recognize this about yourselves, that Jesus Christ is in you – unless indeed you fail the test" (2 Cor 13-5-6)?

If we make a decision to abandon Christ, we would have to question the genuineness of our conversion in the first place. Since Christ lives in us, and since it His responsibility to keep us, then, it seems that He will not let us act out a decision to abandon Him. If our salvation is left up to us, we would fall short every time.

We do have free fill, and we can choose to sin. We might even be in sin "for a season". However, like King David when he sinned, his "heart troubled him" (2 Sam 24:20) and on another occasion "David's conscience bothered him" (1 Sam 24:5).

If indeed the Spirit of the living God lives within us, and He does, though we might try to ignore Him when we are committing sin, we will be under a continued conviction of our sin by the Holy Spirit. A person that can go on sinning willfully without being under any conviction by the Holy Spirit, is a person who must not have the Holy Spirit residing in him or her because, "No one who is born of God practices sin" (1 John 3:9). That is, "no one born of God" can live in an ongoing sinful lifestyle without the kindness of God leading that person back to repentance (Rom 2:4).

Consider this…if you have ever made a decision to follow Christ and you are now questioning the genuineness of this decision, the mere fact that you are reading this might be an indication of God's love and grace holding on to you by continually drawing you to Him.

What If I Commit The "Unpardonable Sin"?

It is the unbeliever who has committed the unpardonable sin by choosing to not believe.

When we understand what the "unpardonable sin" is, we will realize that it is impossible for a genuine believer to commit it. The unpardonable sin is the rejection of Jesus Christ by an unbeliever. A person that dies without having ever received Jesus Christ as Lord and Savior has, thus, committed the unpardonable sin. This is the only sin that will cause someone to spend an eternity apart from Christ.

The term "unpardonable sin" is synonymous with the "blasphemy of the Holy Spirit". Jesus says in Luke 12:10 that "he who blasphemes against the Holy Spirit, it will not be forgiven him". Also, Mark, "But whoever blasphemes against the Holy Spirit never has forgiveness, but is guilty of eternal sin" (Mark 3:28-30). Notice Jesus says one "never has" forgiveness, not "no longer has" forgiveness.

If we look at the context of why Jesus made this statement, it is because the Jews denied who He is. In verse 22, the Scribes claimed that Jesus was casting out demons on behalf of Satan. He explains to them how ludicrous that concept is. Because they said Jesus has "an unclean spirit" (Mark 3:30) (i.e., denying who He is), He is telling them that they are guilty of an "eternal sin" (v. 29).

The story is told by Matthew in a slightly different way; He quotes Jesus, "whoever speaks against the Holy Spirit, it shall not be forgiven him" (Matt 12:32). The word "speak" is often taken by some to mean *curse words* or that somehow it is the words that are important. So, if a genuine believer in a moment of anger or disillusionment with God somehow curses God or says the words "I quit, or I don't want you anymore" that believer has suddenly blasphemed the Holy Spirit and lost his or her salvation. This is not a correct exegesis of Scripture, nor is it a correct view of our Father. Jesus is referring to the lost condition of the heart of the Scribes that put Him in the same category as Satan. In other words, they denied that Jesus is God, the Lord and Savior, the Messiah. If you do not accept who Christ really is, you cannot be saved. Thus, you have committed the eternal, unpardonable sin.

When Paul was "solemnly testifying to the Jews that Jesus was the Christ," the Jews "resisted and blasphemed". They rejected that Paul was teaching about Christ – they, in essence, rejected Christ. Paul drew the line in the sand and, basically, told them they were doomed; "your blood be on your own heads! I am clean. From now on I will go to the Gentiles" (Acts 18:5-6).

Paul told King Agrippa that before Paul was converted; Paul tried to get the Christians to "blaspheme" (Acts 26:11). That is, in context, he tried to get them to speak ill of Christ (though we have no record of Paul being successful in doing so).

James tells the twelve tribes dispersed abroad (James 1:1) that it is a certain group of rich people that "blaspheme the fair names by which you have been called" (James 2:7). Since the believers James is addressing were treating the rich with favoritism (James 2:1-4), it seems safe to assume that these rich folks were appearing to fit in to the congregation. Yet James states they were the blasphemers. He seems to be speaking to the genuine believers and separating the "one's who are blaspheming the noble name of him to whom you belong". That is, this group of blasphemers rejected Christ by their actions and revealed the true attitude of their hearts (v. 6-7).

A genuine believer cannot commit an unpardonable sin. Only if a person never accepts Christ will they have committed the unpardonable sin – the sin of rejecting Christ.

Can I "Fall From Grace" or "Fall Away" From Salvation?

How far must one fall to be considered fallen?

My first question is how far would we have to "fall" to reach the point that we are no longer saved. No one seems to have a legitimate answer to this question. The pat answer is "when we become apostate." When is that? (See page 29)

There are a number of verses in Scripture that refer in some form or another to "falling away". I believe the most blatant is Galatians 5:4, "You have been severed from Christ, you who are seeking to be justified by law; you have fallen from grace". The apparent connection is those who have "fallen from grace" have been "severed" from Christ. So, what does it mean to be "severed" from Christ?

The American Heritage Dictionary defines *sever* as "1. To divide or separate. 2. To cut off (a part) from the whole. 3. To break up (e.g. a relationship): dissolve[8]". Those with a presupposition to a believer losing salvation will naturally gravitate to use the second or third definition. While, admittedly, those on the other side of the debate will gravitate to the first definition.

The Greek definition is similar in its broad descriptions of how the word can be used. The Greek word is *Katargeo* (Strong's #2673) and can mean, "To render idle, unemployed, inactive, inoperative, bring to naught, make of none effect, to cause to cease, put an end to, do away with, annul, abolish, to be severed from, separated from[9]" and so on. Therefore, to determine the correct use of the word, one must determine the context of its use.

In Galatians 5, verse 1, Paul refers to the freedom that believers have in Christ. In verse 2 if a person trusts in the law rather than in Christ, then, he states, "Christ shall profit you nothing" (KJV). In verse 3, he reminds them that they must trust in either Christ or the law. Because if they trust in the law, they must keep the entire law (which we know is impossible).

The King James Version, in this case, is a more literal translation of verse four, "Christ is become of no effect unto whosoever of you *are* justified by law; ye are fallen from grace". Remembering that at any given time, any one of the early churches was no different from any modern church, in that, the congregations consist of genuine believers and pseudo-believers (false believers). Therefore, we must assume that Paul, in writing to the Galatian churches, is writing to mixed audiences. Paul has a habit of challenging those who call themselves "believers" to examine the genuineness of their faith.

Here again, Paul challenges the recipients: Are you a genuine follower of Christ, justified by His grace? Then remember to walk in that grace (live in the spirit – verse 16). Do you believe you will be justified by the law? Then, you have missed the point. Your so-called faith is of "no effect"; it is invalid, of no use. You are separated from Christ because you have yet to be with Him by grace alone through faith, not by law.

A genuine believer cannot be cut-off from salvation; we cannot fall so far we lose the free gift of God. God's gifts and callings are "irrevocable" (Rom 11:29). Again, if we can fall and lose salvation, how far does one have to fall? At what point are we once again hopeless? One might say we lose our salvation at the point that we "blaspheme" the Holy Spirit. However, we know this is impossible (see above). One might say we lose our salvation at the point that we become "apostate". However, we have learned that this term is misused, even abused.

Therefore, we can rest assured that when we fall, Christ will lift us up. In addition, as genuine believers, we should be instrumental in being used by Jesus to help our stumbling brothers and sisters.

What If I Do Not "Endure To The End"?

Endure to the end of what?

We are to "endure to the end" of what, exactly? If we take a verse like, "the one who endures to the end, he will be saved" (Mark 13:13) and couple it with a presupposition that one can lose one's salvation, it would seem to be a strong argument. However, all the references to this statement "endure to the end" are found in the gospels. Moreover, each refers to a specific event or series of events the disciples would be facing. Further, none of the verses refers to the end of one's natural life, which seems to be what our presuppositions lead us to believe.

In the context of these verses (Matt 10:22, 24:13; Mark 13:13, Luke 21:19), Jesus is assuring the disciples that, though there will be tough times coming, the end for them is always bright – they will be saved. As Matthew, Mark and Luke recall the story; Jesus is forewarning his disciples of a forthcoming tribulation period. Some scholars interpret this as the final tribulation period (further defining Pre-Trib, Mid-Trib, or Post-Trib views) coupled with the return of Christ. If this is the case, "enduring to the end" is not applicable to the early disciples any more than it is applicable to those of us who may die before the end-times tribulation. How can we endure to the end of something that we will not ever live through?

Others believe Jesus is referring to the soon coming destruction of the temple and fall of Jerusalem, which occurred, between A.D. 66

and A.D. 70. Jesus states, "not one stone shall be left upon another which will not be torn down" (Mark 13:2). If this is the case, then Jesus is referring to the "end" of the soon coming period of which those listening to his warning will likely take part. It is as though Jesus is saying, "you will be facing tribulation and persecution like never before. Hang in there. Be of good courage knowing that your end is secure, the 'one who endures', the one who is still fighting the good fight has a great reward for his endurance".

Nowhere in context can one interpret this phrase to mean that the one who does *not* endure to the end (of what?) will lose one's salvation. To do so would be to approach the Scripture with a presupposition and read into it what is not there (referred to as eisegesis).

There is one other possibility, which would also fall in line with Christ's teachings about "knowing them by their fruits" (Matt 7:16). That is, He could be telling the disciples that the upcoming persecutions will separate the wheat from the chaff – the genuine believers from the false ones (Luke 3:17). Those who do not endure to the end of the upcoming tribulation period might not be genuine believers. This, however, is also an inference not specifically stated in these verses. We are safest to take Christ's words at face value, that those who endure the upcoming tribulation period (again, whenever it may be) will be saved.

Please do not be tempted to let your presupposition or bias interpret this scripture to mean the end of one's natural life. This concept is not found in scripture.

What If My Name Gets Erased From The Book Of Life?

If the book of life is synonymous with salvation, and our names are written in it from the beginning, exactly when would they be erased?

We ask, what is this Book of Life? Whose names are in it? How did those names get there? When did they get there? Can they be removed? The key verse used for the argument that one can lose one's salvation by having one's name erased from the Book of Life is Revelation 3:5:

> "He who overcomes will thus be clothed in white garments; and I will not erase his name from the Book of Life, and I will confess his name before My Father and before His angels".

Let us first examine when our names are found in the Book of Life. Revelation 17:8 indicates that our names are either in or out of God's book from the very beginning:

> "And those who dwell on the earth, whose name has not been written in the Book of Life *from the foundation of the world*" (emphasis added).

In addition, Jesus comforts His disciples, "but rejoice that your names *are* recorded in heaven" (Luke 10:20), emphasis added). He simply states the fact that their names *are* recorded. He does not tell us when. However, from the verse in Revelation 17, and with a little insight about God's foreknowledge, we can safely assume that God knows from the beginning who will and who will not be saved.

In Exodus, Moses refers to God having a "book". However, he does not use the term "Book of Life". It could be the book of

Remembrance (Mal 3:16)? Could all the books be the same? Either way, did God write at the "foundation of the world" the names of all those who are in the book or not? One more thought, if God is a Spirit (John 4:24), then does He have a real book as we think of books? On the other hand, is the "book" more of a natural term used to describe a spiritual principle that God knows who are His?

Charles Stanley writes, "The ancient Hebrews viewed God as a great record keeper. They pictured Him having in His possession a book with a list of all *living* people… anyone who has read much of the Old Testament knows that names and genealogies were very important to the Jews, who took this type of record keeping very serious[10]" (emphasis added).

So, is God's book (or books) metaphoric for God's knowledge of human history? Moses and David both use the term when referring to our natural lives or our deeds (see Exodus 32:32-33, Ps 87:6, 51:1, 56:8, 69:28, 139:15-16).

Finally, referring again to Revelation 3:5, the authors' use of the word "not" (I will not erase) is a double negative Greek word *ou me* (Strong's #3364). This double negative emphasis means "never ever, not at all, by no means". It is a strong denial implying an utter impossibility. Spiros Zodhiates defines this word as "a double negative strengthening the denial; not at all – any more, at all, by any (no) means, neither, never, no (at all), in no case (wise), nor ever, not (at all, in any way wise)[11]".

In conclusion, the genuine believer will have his or her name in the Book of Life from the foundation of the world and it will not be removed, in no way, for any reason. The Lord "knows those who are His" (2 Tim 2:19)!

Note: the fact that our names are written in the book of life from the beginning of time calls for a completely separate study on that topic. It has no bearing on the above discussion.

Section Summary

We have now learned what one must *understand* to be saved, what one must *do* to be saved and what it *looks* like to be saved. We also should have a great assurance of our salvation if we *are* truly saved.

As we close this study, let us encourage those who have taken a sincere look in the mirror and are now wrestling with whether or not they are really saved.

If you have had any experiences with Christianity, but do not feel like you have born any fruit of conversion, God is not finished with you. He has been leading you to Him. Every trip to the altar you have taken, every Bible study you have attended, has been the work of the Holy Spirit in preparing your heart for such a time as this.

If now you have counted the costs, and you are ready to yield your will to His, simply let Jesus know. Like the tax collector, cry out for the Lord to have mercy on you, a sinner.

You can get on your knees right now as an act of humility and ask Jesus Christ to forgive all of your sins (see the prayer on page 22).

Tell Him that by His grace and with your will submitted that you will no longer live for yourself but will serve and worship Him alone as Lord and Savior.

Receive by faith His forgiveness and believe in your heart that He is the God who bore your sins on the cross. Hallelujah!

If you have made a genuine commitment to Jesus, tell as many people as possible, as soon as possible, about your decision to live for Christ! If you are too embarrassed to tell those who know you best, you may still not be ready.

For those who are genuine believers but have wavered in your security of that fact, I trust that you are now encouraged. Make a decision that you will no longer waiver in your faith, and you will make any adjustments necessary in your walk with Christ, to make your life be glorifying to God. As Paul puts it, "If we live by the Spirit, let us also walk by the Spirit" (Gal 5:25). In addition, "Let us not lose heart in doing good, for in due time we will reap if we do not grow weary" (Gal 6:9).

APPENDIX

I've included my research for all the scriptures in question. Each verse was prayerfully and carefully studied using commonly approached reference works and employing hermeneutics – the study of ancient biblical texts.

Each verse is written out in the two primary versions used in my study: New American Standard Bible (NASB) and King James Version (KJV).

I endeavored to provide some context for the verse based on both the context of the chapter or chapters surrounding the verse and historical context when applicable.

The comments are my thoughts and questions as well as some of the results of my research. My comments are provided here to help you do your own research with an understanding of what I was thinking during mine. I hope these comments will also provide a framework for studying all of scripture.

I provide what I believe to be a summation or determination of whether or not the verse supports what I am referring to as eternal security – the main issue at large. There should only be three potential observations in the summation: 1) the verse opposes eternal security; 2) the verse supports eternal security; or, 3) the verse is neutral and, therefore, neither opposes nor supports eternal security. I was pleasantly surprised by the results. You will be too.

I then provide a further explanation when needed. These are more observations discovered from the research.

I tried to outline the opposing view, if there is one, to the concept of eternal security. In other words, this view would be that one can lose their salvation. I studied several books that attempted to support this view to find out what their arguments would be and to see if scripture supported those arguments. Though some of the arguments in the opposing view might make philosophical or logical sense, they turned out to not be supported by the verse that was quoted. Not all verses quoted here have an opposing view.

Finally, I provide my conclusion to the study of the verse.

This study took approximately 1000 hours over the course of nearly three years to complete. Each one of these verses and subjects were painstakingly studied with as much of an open mind and a keen awareness of my potential biases as humanly possible.

Something I was cognizant about and had to be careful about was that during the course of my studies I began to see a pattern arising. I worked hard to remain neutral in my opinions so that I could remain true to doing an exegetical study. I did not want the forming of a bias to skew the results of individual verse studies. I was determined to seek and accept the truth regardless of the position it unveiled.

The appendix verses are listed in the order in which they appear in the Bible.

Exodus 32:32-33

> NASB: "But now, if you will, forgive their sin – and, if not, please blot me out from Your book which you have written!' The Lord said to Moses, 'whoever has sinned against Me, I will blot him out of My book'".

> KJV: Yet now, of thou wilt forgive their sin; - and if not, blot me, I pray thee, out of Thy book which Thou hast written. And the Lord said unto Moses, whosoever hath sinned against me, him will I blot out of my book".

Context: Moses had come down the mountain to find that the people had made a golden calf and were dancing. They had sinned against the Lord. Moses asks the Lord to forgive their sin. If not, to blot Moses from the book the Lord had written.

Comments:
- The question is "what book"? There is no apparent connection to the Book of Life mentioned in Philippians or Revelation.
- Verse 34 has God saying He will punish them for their sin
- Verse 35 has the Lord smiting the people. "Smote" is the Hebrew word "*nagaph*" (Strong's $5062). Zodhiates defines it… "This word is a blow which is fatal or disastrous… The term was used of the Lord striking men with some plague, sickness or death…"

Summation: This verse is neither for nor against eternal security.

Further Explanation: It would appear that this verse has nothing to do with a believers' salvation. It strictly refers to punishing the Israelites for their rebellion – a punishment that could lead to physical death. This passage is simply a historical narrative demonstrating God killing certain Israelites for turning to idols and not repenting.

Opposing View: Some might say that this verse supports Revelation 3:5 in that it shows that God does indeed blot people out of the "Book of Life" (See Revelation 3:5 review).

Conclusion: The dilemma with this opposing view is that this verse only refers to a "book", not the "Book of Life". There are several books mentioned in Scripture; Book of Life, Thy Book, and Book of Remembrance. It is not clear if this is one of those books or an altogether different book. We also consider that the concept of God even having "books" is symbolic since God is Spirit (non-corporeal) and the term "book" may just be symbolic of some greater truth. In this case, removing the people from "Thy Book" is referring to God taking the lives of those who have rebelled. One cannot honestly assume this means eternal life. To do so is to read in to Scripture what is not being said in context.

Psalm 51:10-12.

> NASB: "Create in me a clean heart, O God and renew a right Spirit within me. Do not cast me away from Your presence. And do not take your Holy Spirit from me. Restore me to the joy of your salvation and sustain me with a willing spirit."

> KJV: Create in me a clean heart, O God; and renew a right spirit within me. Cast me not away from thy presence; and take not thy Holy Spirit from me. Restore unto me the joy of thy salvation; and uphold me with thy free spirit."

Context: David is praying after having been convicted of his sin of adultery with Bathsheba and murder of her husband. He is praying for a restoration of his intimacy with his God, an intimacy that was broken by his sinful acts.

Comments:
- David understood the holy life. He understood what it meant to have constant communion with God's spirit.

- His cry here is to have that restored. He wants to return to the steadfast state he used to have.
- He knows that sin breaks fellowship with the Holy Spirit and he longs for that fellowship to return. His desire is to experience again the joy of salvation that comes from God.
- In verse 14 he states clearly his understanding that salvation is of the Lord and that David is saved as he said, "the God of *my* salvation" (emphasis added).

Opposing View: Based on his use of the phrase, "take not Your Holy Spirit from me", the opposing view is that David was concerned with and aware that he could lose his salvation. To say this is to read in to Scripture what is not there.

Conclusion: God favors a broken and contrite heart. If we have salvation and sin breaks our fellowship, God will restore our fellowship when we repent. As grievous a sin as it was that David committed, he is still referred to in Scripture as a man after God's own heart.

Matthew 7:22-23

> NASB: "Many will say to me on that day, 'Lord, Lord, did we not prophesy in Your name, and in Your name cast out demons, and in Your name perform miracles?' And, then I will declare to them, 'I never knew you; depart from Me, you who practice lawlessness'".

> KJV: "Many will say to me in that day, 'Lord, Lord, have we not prophesied in thy name? And in thy name have cast out devils? And in thy name done many wonderful works?' And then will I profess unto them, 'I never knew you: depart from me, ye that work iniquity'".

Context: Jesus just finished telling his people to beware of false prophets. Then he addresses this group of people. Apparently, these are the ones who do "works" in Christ's name but who have no personal, saving relationship with Him.

Comments:
- The significant phrase here is that Christ "never" knew the people who professed to be His.

Summation: *This verse is neither for nor against eternal security.*

Further Explanation: These false prophets (or pseudo-Christians) may have thought they were in Christ's good graces. However, they did not understand His grace at all. Based on the surprise in their comments, they must have believed their good works would earn His favor. Yet, Christ *never* knew them.

Opposing View: Some people try to use this passage to show that we can never be sure of our salvation. After all, might we not be deceiving ourselves and therefore find ourselves in the same boat as those mentioned in the passage?

Conclusion: However, Christ *never knew* this group of people. Yet, He fully knows those who are His, and He speaks to them. His followers hear His voice and follow Him. A genuine believer is saved by *grace* through *faith* alone – not by good works. Works, no matter how good or in whose name, will never put us in a right relationship with Christ.

Matthew 22:14

NASB: "For many are called, but few are chosen".

KJV: "For many are called, but few are chosen".

Context: Jesus is telling a parable of the wedding feast. He is speaking directly to the chief Priests and the Pharisees. This parable is a simile "the kingdom of heaven [is like] may be compared to…"

Comments:
- The Greek word for "called" is *Kletos* (Strong's #2822). Thayer's states: "invited (by God in the proclamation of the Gospel) to obtain eternal salvation in the kingdom of God through Christ. Called, Invited.
- The Greek word for "chosen" is *eklektos* (Strong's #1588). Thayer's states: "Picked out, chosen. Chosen by God, (a) to obtain salvation through Christ; those who have become true partakers of the Christian salvation are contrasted with "kletos", those who have been invited but who have not shown themselves fitted to obtain it 'others regard the 'called' and 'chosen' here as alike partakers of salvation, but the latter as the 'choice' ones, distinguished above the former'".
- This parable is about the Jews as a 'chosen race' having the offer of salvation made to them. However, since this general group did not accept the invitation, Jesus demonstrates that He then broadens the invitation to the Gentiles. The new guests are invited without regard to their evil or good deeds. One guest, however, did not have a change of clothing (heart) and was bound and thrown out of the feast. Outside the feast is weeping and great despair.
- "Many" were invited to accept the offer of salvation by grace. However, only a "few" actually accepted the salvation and were changed by it.

Summation: This verse is neither for nor against eternal security.

Further Explanation: This parable demonstrates that Christ calls or invites many to salvation. However, only those who have a change of heart become God's chosen people.

Opposing View: There is the potential to read in to this text that everyone was saved who were in the wedding hall. Then, the one who was found not dressed in wedding clothes subsequently "lost" his salvation. However, there is no indication that he had first put on "wedding clothes" and then removed them. Therefore, there is no association available here to say that we are saved but can still be "bound and thrown out" of the feast. It is more likely that this person was a "tare among the wheat (Matt 13\:30).

Conclusion: This passage best demonstrates that genuine believers are distinct from pseudo-believers and that Christ knows His own.

Mark 13:13

> NASB: "You will be hated by all because of My name, but the one who endures to the end, he will be saved".

> KJV: "And ye shall be hated of all men for my name's sake: but he that shall endure to the end, the same shall be saved".

Context: Some of the disciples were sitting with Jesus looking at the Temple (v 1-3). Jesus begins a discourse about the signs of the times – the upcoming tribulation and the end of the world. He gives them a message of comfort and hope as they face the forthcoming tribulations.

Comments:
- Jesus describes, starting in verse 9, the persecution his disciples would face. He also tells how the temple and Jerusalem will be destroyed – which happened in A.D. 70.
- He refers to this "tribulation period" which will be the greatest time of tribulation ever known. He describes things that will happen, "in those days, after the tribulation", (v. 24).
- He also explains the timing by stating, "this generation will not pass way until all these things take place" (v. 30). Apparently, this refers to the tribulation period and all that is described with it. If the tribulation Jesus referred to was, in fact, the period of A.D. 64 – A.D. 70 under the persecution of Nero and successor, Vespasian, and the destruction of the Temple by Titus, the son of Vespasian, then Jesus' comment about this generation not passing away makes sense without having to spiritualize the term "generation" to mean something else.

- He then says "heaven and earth will pass away… that day or hour no one knows" (v. 31). This statement refers to the finality of all things. The earlier tribulation He referred to is not the end, for it is said to be the "beginning of birth pangs" (v. 48).
- Regardless of when this tribulation period is to take place (or has taken place), we would all agree that the reference in verse 13 is to those who endure to the end of the tribulation period.

Summation: This verse "indirectly" provides for our assurance of salvation.

Further Explanation: We must honestly ask the question: endure to the end of what? Endure to the end of our natural lives? Endure to the end of the tribulation period? It cannot be inferred to mean "the end of our natural lives".

Opposing View: The only way to use this verse to support a view of being able to lose one's salvation is to say that one must "endure to the end" of one's natural life. (i.e., remain *in faith* until we die). However, the context of this passage does not support this argument. In addition, the passage does not give any information as to what will happen to those believers who do not endure to the end of the tribulation period described. It is feasible that this or any tribulation period will separate the wheat from the chaff, the genuine from the false believers.

Conclusion: In context, this passage provides a promise to those believers who endured (or will endure) tribulation. We can apply this same promise to us today, in that, though we go through tribulations, we have salvation as our final hope. Heaven awaits the genuine believer.

Luke 6:46-49

NASB: "Why do you call Me, 'Lord, Lord,' and do not do what I say?' Everyone who comes to Me and hears My words and acts on them, I will show you whom he is like: he is like a man building a house, who dug deep and laid a foundation on the rock; and when a flood occurred, the torrent burst against the house and could not shake it, because it had been well built. But the one who has heard and has not acted accordingly, is like a man who built a house on the ground without any foundation; and the torrent burst against it and immediately it collapsed, and the ruin of that house was great."

KJV: "and why call ye me, Lord, Lord, and do not the things which I say? Whosoever cometh to me, and heareth my sayings, and doeth them, I will show you to whom he is like: He is like a man which built an house, and digged deep, and laid the foundation on a rock: and when the flood arose, the stream beat vehemently upon that house, and could not shake it: for it was founded upon a rock. But he that heareth, and doeth not, is like a man that without foundation built an house upon the earth: against which the stream did beat vehemently, and immediately it fell; and the ruin of that house was great".

Context: Jesus is using a simile to describe the difference between the genuine believer and the false believer.

Comments:
- Everyone who; 1) comes to Christ; 2) hears His words; and 3) does what He says, is the one who has Christ in his cornerstone or foundation. Those who claim to have Christ as Lord but do not obey Him are not His at all. They never built on Him as their foundation.

Summation: This verse provides assurance for our eternal security.

Further Explanation: This passage makes a clear delineation between those who do and those who do not belong to Christ. One either has a foundation or not.

Opposing View: This view would say that Christians who do not do what Christ says are like the ones that built their foundation on the ground. However, the foundation is built once before the house is built. One cannot go back and change the foundation under the house.

Conclusion: When one builds one's foundation upon Christ, the foundation will stand the torrents of life that come against it. However, when one builds one's foundation upon anything but Christ, that one will not have the security of Christ or of eternal life with Him. In fact, it may well be the torrents of life that will eventually identify the pseudo-believer. If one builds one's faith on Christ, then that faith will stand.

Luke 8:13

> NASB: "And those on the rocky soil are those who, when they hear, receive the word with joy; and these have no firm root; they believe for a while, and in time of temptation fall away".

> KJV: "They on the rock are they, which, when they hear, receive the word with joy; and these have no root, which for a while believe, and in time of temptation fall away".

Context: This passage is part of the parable of the Sower (or the Soils). This verse is specifically referring to the second seed that fell on the rocky soil. The parallel passages are Matthew 13:20-21, and Mark 4:16-17.

Comments:
- The immediate question arises because of Luke's use of the term "fall away". This is the Greek word *aphistantai* (from the root "*aphistemi*" (Strong's #868). In reference to the specific passage Spiros Zodhiates states, "The word *aphistantai* here does not indicate uprooting because there never was a root; the temporary plant stood by itself. The union with the soil was only an apparent union, never a true foundation with roots

capable of holding up the plant[12]" It is further defined by Thayer's as, "to withdraw one's self from: absolutely fall away[13]".

- Aside from the Greek word definitions, as honest exegetical evaluation of the passage explains that "these have no firm root (NASB)"; and "these have no root (KJV)" and the statement in the Interlinear Bible states, "and these root do not have[14]". Therefore, the ones whose soil was rocky actually had no root, no firm foundation on the Rock (see Luke 6:46-49).

Summation: This verse is neither for nor against eternal security.

Further Explanation: These people may have had an appearance of a plant or branch (Christian), but they never were attached to the vine Himself. They will eventually give up since *trying* to remain a "Christian" (as they believe they are) is too difficult without Jesus being the firm foundation and the torrents will eventually collapse what they have built.

Opposing View: One might think that because these people heard His voice and became joyful, that they were then saved. Then, later because of temptations, they "fell away" and lost their salvation. To say this is to ignore the primary issue of whether or not these people actually had a foundation in Christ at all.

Conclusion: Whom this verse is describing are those who have a form of godliness, but deny its power; the false Christians.

Luke 10:20

> NASB; "Nevertheless do not rejoice in this, that the spirits are subject to you, but rejoice that your names are recorded in heaven".

KJV: "Notwithstanding in this rejoice not, that the spirits are subject unto you; but rather rejoice, because your names are written in heaven".

Context: The seventy disciples were rejoicing that the spirits were subject to their authority. Christ refocuses them on the more important fact that their names are recorded in heaven.

Comments:
- It is interesting to note the Lord's opening comment in verse eighteen: "And He said to them, 'I was watching Satan fall from heaven like lightning'". This seems to be an allusion to Isaiah 14:12; "How you have fallen from heaven…" in reference to Satan. It is almost as if Christ is telling the disciples, just as I was watching Satan fall at the beginning of history, I had already given you authority to tread upon him. So, do not get excited about the demons being subject to you. In fact, be excited that at the beginning of history (at the time I was watching Satan fall from heaven), I already recorded your names in heaven (or possibly in the Book of Life). Whether or not that is what He meant, the simplicity of this passage is that the disciples' names *are* recorded in heaven, which seems to be the same concept of being written in the Book of Life.
- In verse twenty alone, there is no reference as to when the names were recorded, just that they indeed, are, recorded.
- "Recorded" in the Greek is a verb in the "Perfect Indicative Passive" tense, which refers to an action, completed in the past that has continuing results.
-

Summation: This verse is neither for not against eternal security.

Further Explanation: This passage is merely a reference to the fact that believers have their names written in heaven. "Written in heaven" may have some connection to "written in the Book of Life", though this is not specifically stated.

Opposing View: The argument would be that the phrase "written in heaven" is synonymous with the Book of Life in which case, the names can be blotted out according to Revelation 3:5. (*See above, What If My Name Gets Erased From The Book Of Life?*)

Conclusion: Genuine believers can rejoice that their names "are" written in heaven!

Luke 13:23-28

> NASB: "And someone said to Him, 'Lord, are there just a few who are being saved?' And He said to them, 'Strive to enter through the narrow door; for many, I tell you, will seek to enter and will not be able'. Once the head of the house gets up and shuts the door, and you begin to stand outside and knock on the door, saying, 'Lord, open up to us!' then he will answer and say to you, 'I do not know where you are from'. Then you will begin to say, 'we ate and drank in Your presence, and You taught in our streets; and he will say, 'I tell you, I do not know where you are from; depart from Me, all you evildoers.' In that place there will be weeping and gnashing of teeth when you see Abraham and Isaac and Jacob and all the prophets in the kingdom of God, but yourselves being thrown out".

> KJV: "Then said one unto him, Lord, are there a few that be saved? And he said unto them, strive to enter in at the strait gate: for many, I say unto you, will seek to enter in, and shall not be able. When once the master of the house is risen up, and hath shut the door, and ye begin to stand without, and to knock at the door, saying, Lord, Lord, open unto us; and he shall answer and say unto you, I know yo"u not whence ye are: then shall ye begin to say, we have eaten and drunk in thy presence, and thou has taught in our streets. But he shall say, I tell you, I know you not whence ye are: depart from me, all ye workers of iniquity. There shall be weeping and gnashing of teeth. When ye shall see Abraham, and Isaac, and Jacob, and all the

prophets, in the kingdom of God, and you yourselves thrust
out."

Context: Jesus tells a parable of a head of household not allowing
evildoers to enter through the door once it has been shut. They claim to
have a relationship with him. However, he says he does not know
where they are from.

Comments:
- The parable is dyadic – having only two characters: the head of
  the household and those who are trying to get in – the
  evildoers. The parable is about salvation.
- Jesus is speaking to Jews since they would not understand his
  comments in verse 28 about seeing Abraham, Isaac, Jacob and
  all the prophets.
- The main point of the parable is, a personal relationship with
  the master is required – not just a casual knowledge of or
  acquaintance with him.
- "Gnashing" is the Greek word *brugmos* (Strong's #1030)
  Gnashing of teeth is "a phrase denoting the extreme anguish
  and utter despair of men consigned to eternal condemnation[15]".
- This parable only describes being inside or outside the house.
  If you are not inside with the master, then you are outside
  (presumably in the streets – the utter darkness) where there will
  be weeping and utter despair. It says nothing directly of a
  separate place of hell.

Summation: This verse is neither for nor against eternal security.

Further Explanation: This passage describes the need for a personal
relationship with Christ. It is not enough to be a church going person,
to know the word of God, or even to teach the word of God. One must
personally be known by Jesus or one will not even so much as enter
into the kingdom of God.

Opposing View: Some say that these are believers who are living
wickedly. As a result, they are "thrust out" of the kingdom of God

because of their wicked deeds. However, a careful study of the passage will show that these *evildoers* "will seek to enter and will not be able". These evildoers never actually entered in. Although, they themselves thought they had entered because of some association with the master.

Conclusion: A person is either in or out of the kingdom of God and not based on their deeds, but based on whether or not the master knows the individual personally. This passage should give reason to pause and reflect on one's relationship to the Master.

John 4:13-14

> NASB: "Jesus answered and said to her, 'everyone who drinks of this water will thirst again; but whoever drinks of the water that I will give him shall never thirst; but the water that I will give him will become in him a well of water springing up to eternal life'".

> KJV: "Jesus answered and said unto her, whosoever drinketh of this water shall thirst again: But whosoever drinketh of the water that I shall give him shall never thirst; but the water that I shall give him shall be in him a well of water springing up into everlasting life".

Context: Jesus stopped at a well in Sychar, a city of Samaria, on His way to Galilee. He is speaking to a Samaritan woman. He uses the water in the well as an analogy to Him being the water of life. He promises eternal life upon the condition of drinking His water.

Comments:
- The keywords here are the two uses of "drinks" and the use of "thirst" in verse 14.
- In verse 13, "drinks" is the present participle indicating a continuous action. This is the reference to the physical drinking of a natural water to sustain physical life. When we stop this

type of drinking, we quickly become thirsty even to the point of natural death if we refuse to drink.

- In verse 14, "drinks" is in the aorist subjunctive verb tense. This indicates that the action of drinking has been completed. There is no regard for the duration or continuous action as in the present participle. It also does not indicate when the action takes place. Further, as a subjunctive, it indicates the action is not "sure" to take place.

- Moreover, in verse 14, the Emphatic Future Negative form of the verb "thirst" (shall never thirst) means that if the person drinks (aorist subjunctive) His water, they will definitely not ever thirst again.

Summation: This verse provides assurance for our eternal security.

Further Explanation: Taking into full consideration the verb tenses used, it would seem that once one comes to a genuine, saving faith in Christ and takes action to receive Him as Lord and Savior (i.e., drinking His water), one remains quenched of the thirst for eternal life.

Opposing View: The other argument is that one must continue drinking the water of life in order to remain saved. If one stops drinking, then one becomes lost. This argument, then, must ignore the use in the text of the different verb tenses. Again, at what point would one be considered to have stopped "drinking"?

Conclusion: This passage provides an encouraging support that once a person takes a drink of the water of life, that person will never again become thirsty. In other words, once a person is genuinely converted to Christ, that person remains His.

John 5:24

NASB: "Truly, truly, I say to you, he who hears My word, and believes Him who sent Me, has eternal life, and does not come to into judgment, but has passed out of death into life".

KJV: "Verily, verily, I say unto you, he that heareth my word, and believeth him that sent me, hath everlasting life, and shall not come into condemnation; but is passed from death until life".

Context: Jesus is in Jerusalem being confronted by and persecuted by the Jews for healing on the Sabbath. In addition, and more importantly, He is being persecuted for making Himself out to be equal to God. Jesus indicates the importance of hearing His words and believing in His Father. He promises to those who meet this qualification that they will not come into judgment, that they have eternal life and that they have passed from death to life.

Comments:
- There are three keywords to consider in the context: *hears*, *believes*, and has *passed*.
    o Hears (My word) and Believes (Him) are both "present participles" in the Geek language. The verb tenses here indicate a continuous or repeated action but do not indicate the time of the action. The main verb in the text helps to identify the timing.
    o Passed (out of death) is a "perfect indicative" which indicates an event that has taken place in the past but continues into the present and is stated emphatically as being actual, factual or real.

Summation: This verse provides assurance for our eternal security.

Further Explanation: Those who presently hear and believe in the father and son are promised they now have eternal life, will not come into judgment and have passed from being spiritually dead to now being spiritually alive.

Opposing View: Some focus on the "present participle" of the word and believer and therefore state that one must "continue believing" in order to "maintain" salvation. However, one cannot set apart a single word and build or support a doctrine on that word. The verb "passed" (out of death) indicates that once a person comes to the point of genuine believing, that person then receives eternal life and has now passed or crossed the threshold from death to life. It cannot be said of the passage that as long as a person keeps believing that that person continues to pass from death and continues to have eternal death.

Conclusion: Once a person believes, that person then passes from death to life once and for all. The issue of continuously believing is resolved through the whole council of God's word in that Christ is the one ultimately able to "make us stand" (Jude 24) blameless in his presence.

John 6:39-40

> NASB: "This is the will of Him who sent Me, that of all that He has given Me I lose nothing, but raise it up on the last day. For this is the will of My Father, that everyone who beholds the Son and believes in Him will have eternal life, and I Myself will raise him up on the last day".

> KJV: "And this is the father's will which has sent me, that of all which he hath given me I should lose nothing, but should raise it up again at the last day. And this is the will of him that sent me, that every one which seeth the Son, and believeth on him, may have everlasting life: and I will raise him up at the last day".

Context: Jesus is speaking to the crowds that had witnessed Him feeding the multitudes. He explains He is the bread from His Father. That the Father will give the Son a people and it is the will of the Father that the Son loses none of them. Jesus promises those who believe that He will raise them up on the last day. He also promises this eternal life to all who see and believe in Jesus.

<u>Comments</u>:
- It is the Father's will that Jesus does not "lose" any of the people that the Father gives Him.
- "Lose" is the Greek word *apollumi* (Strong's #622) which means to kill, destroy, perish or lose. It is used in verse 39 in the aorist subjunctive tense. So then, in context it is a directive from the Father concerning something specific that the Father does not want to happen but has not happened yet. Christ has not lost anyone – and is to make sure He does not in the future lose anyone.
- All whom He has, He keeps and raises them in the final resurrection (the last day).
- In verse 40, the keywords "behold" and "believes" are in the Present Participle tense indicating a continuous action but with no reference to the timing of the action. The main verb "have" dictates the timing. Those who come to the point of "beholding" and "believing" *have* eternal life. "Have" is used in the Present Subjunctive Active tense which means to currently and continually possess without respect to the timing. Therefore, in coming to the point of believing, one now has and continues to have eternal life.

<u>Summation</u>: This verse provides assurance for our eternal security.

<u>Further Explanation</u>: Once a person truly believes that person now has eternal life – which is immediately experienced, and will forever be experienced. One has the assurance that Christ will raise one in the final resurrection at the second coming.

<u>Opposing View</u>: If Jesus is supposed to lose not even one of His, then why did He lose Judas? There is evidence that Judas never converted his heart. Though he was among the disciples, he demonstrated that he was greedy and self-centered instead of Christ-converted. When the persecution began, Judas showed his true allegiance by betraying Christ and turning Him over to the authorities.

Conclusion: Once we come to the point of believing, we immediately receive the benefit of eternal life. Moreover, we have the assurance that Christ will ensure our resurrection on the last day.

John 8:30-32

> NASB: "As He spoke these things, many came to believe in Him, Jesus therefore was saying to those Jews who had believed Him, 'if you abide in My word, then you are truly disciples of Mine; and you shall know the truth, and the truth shall make you free".
>
> KJV: "As he spake these words, many believed on him. Then said Jesus to those Jews which believed on him, if ye continue in my word, then are ye my disciples indeed; and ye shall know the truth, and the truth shall make you free".

Context: Jesus had been teaching some Jews about believing in Him. As He spoke, many came to believe (v. 30). Then He addresses the ones who did believe in Him.

Comments:
- In the larger context of the passage, verse 44 has Jesus telling this same group of people that their father is the devil. This brings in to question the genuineness of this groups' belief in Him.
- It appears that His use of the word "If" (you abide) also brings in to question whether the "many [who] believed in Him" actually were converted.
- If the genuineness of their conversion is in question, then Jesus may simply be explaining what a genuine believer will look like. I.e., one who is truly converted will abide in His word.
- John seems to further address this issue in his first epistle when he states, "they went out from us, but they were not really of us; for if they had been of us, they would have remained with us" (1 John 2:19).

Summation: This verse provides assurance for our eternal security

Further Explanation: Those who are truly His disciples will prove this out by abiding in His word. One who claims to be a disciple but has no interest in abiding in His word is a "liar and the truth is not in him[16]"

Opposing View: If one stops "abiding" in the word, one becomes lost again; abiding then, in this case, means to continually stay in God's word. However, if reading or studying God's word is the requirement for keeping one's salvation, what did the early Christians do before Paul's or the others' letters were written; What about those believers who are illiterate; What about the deaf and the blind? Being faithful with God's word is important for our spiritual growth. However, the act itself of abiding in the word (the Bible), cannot be the measuring stick for our continued salvation.

Conclusion: Christ shows us that someone who is genuinely converted to Him has a hunger for Him. They abide in Him and He abides in them (see also John 15:2, Pg 64)

John 10:27-28

NASB: "My sheep hear My voice, and I know them, and they follow Me: and I give eternal life to them, and they will never perish; and no one will snatch them out of My hand".

KJV: "My sheep hear my voice, and I know them, and they follow me; and I give unto them eternal life; and they shall never perish, neither shall any many pluck them out of my hand".

Context: Jesus when walking in the temple in the portico of Solomon was confronted by the Jews. He contrasts that only His sheep hear His voice – the Jews were not of His sheep. He appears to be proclaiming that His sheep are permanently His.
Comments:

- Those who have become believers will hear and follow the lord. To those who are His sheep (believers) He gives eternal life and promises they will never perish.
- "Perish" is the Emphatic Future Negative verb tense (like in Revelation 3:5) meaning the believer will absolutely emphatically never perish.
- He further states that no one (or no man) has the ability to snatch a believer away from the father or Christ.
- "Snatch" in the Future tense verb meaning that it would be a future occurrence. However, in this case, "no one" can do it.

Summation: _This verse provides assurance for our eternal security._

Further Explanation: Those who have eternal life (those who hear His voice and follow Him), will never – ever perish. No one can cause them to perish. No one can take a believer away from the Father.

Opposing View: Though there might be no argument that a person cannot be snatched from the Father, it does not say that a person cannot leave the Father on his or her own initiative. If a person willfully quits "hearing" and "following" Christ, that person will lose their salvation. However, one does not find an "if, then" statement in this passage. Jesus is not saying, "_If_ my sheep hear my voice, _then_ they will have eternal life". His sheep _do_ hear his voice, He _does_ know them, and they _will_ follow Him – statements of fact with no room for negotiation.

Conclusion: Genuine believers hear the voice of Jesus and follow Him. Jesus knows those who are His. This passage demonstrates what a genuine believer looks like and provides great assurance to those who are saved.

John 15:2, 6

> NASB: "Every branch in Me that does not bear fruit, He takes away; and every branch that bears fruit, He prunes it, that it may bear more fruit... If anyone does not abide in Me, he is thrown away as a branch, and dries up; and they gather them, and cast them into the fire, and they are burned".

> KJV: "Every branch in me that beareth not fruit he taketh away: and every branch that beareth fruit, he purgeth it, that it may bring forth more fruit... If a man abide not in me he is cast forth as a branch, and is withered; and men gather them, and cast them into the fire, and they are burned."

Context: Throughout chapters 14, 15, and 16, Jesus is comforting His chosen disciples – the Apostles (15:16). He is explaining His forthcoming departure and assuring them of His relationship to them and their relationship to Him, the Father and the Holy Spirit in chapter 15, verses one through eleven, He uses a personification of the vice and the branches to further describe the relationship between himself and His followers.

Comments:
- The primary questions here are :1) Is this set of passages a warning to true believers to "continue" to "abide" in Christ or they will be, as castaways, burned in the fires of hell. 2) Is this an example to demonstrate who the true believers are?
- John is demonstrating through Christ's words in chapter 14, verses 15 and 23 that the one who [claims] to love Jesus is the one who proves this love by his actions. To this person the triune God makes His abode (14:23). We know from the entirety of Scripture that this is not referring to salvation by works. Verse 23 shows that the Spirit of God comes at a specific point in time and inhabits or takes up residence in the heart of the new believer. It is not saying that the Spirit of God lives in us (abides in us) only as keep his commandments.

When we break the commandments, He moves out. Then when we repent, He moves back in.

- The term "abode" (Greek word *mone* [Strong's #3438] means: "to remain, dwell. A mansion, habitation, abode[17]". The Lord makes His permanent dwelling with those who believe. This act of inhabitation is a one-time event.
- The term "abide" in chapter 15:4 means: "In the mystic phraseology of john, God is said [to abide] in Christ, i.e., to dwell as it were within him, to be continually operative in him by his divine influence and energy, Jn 14:10; Christians are said [to abide], to be rooted as it were in him, knit to him by the spirit they have received from Him, 1 John 2:6, 24, 27; 3:6; hence one is said [to abide] in Christ or God, and conversely Christ or God is said [to abide] in one: John 6:56; 15:4; 1 John 3:24; 4:13, 16[18]"
- John 15:5 explains the one who abides is the one who bears fruit. Verse 6, the one who does not bear fruit is the one who does not abide. Verse 8 sums up John's writing and Jesus' message: the one who bears fruit proves themselves to be true disciples.
- John further elaborates on his theology of distinguishing the true believer from the false in his epistles. His first letter, (chapter 2:19), states, "they were not really of us; for if they had been of us, they would have *remained* (Greek word *Menos* [Strong's #3306] – same as John 15:4) with us; but they went out, in order that it might be shown that they all are not of us",

Summation: This verse is neither for nor against eternal security.

Further Explanation: This passage provides us an example by which we can test the genuineness of our faith in Christ. Do we bear fruit that demonstrates genuine repentance?

Opposing View: This argument is that the branch must be first attached to the vine in order to be removed. The verse starts with "every branch in Me". Therefore, these must be genuine believers (attached to the vine), that because of their fruitless lives were removed and sent to hell. However, Christ further explains the statement when he goes on to say "if anyone does not abide in Me". To abide in Christ is to have a personal relationship with Him.

Conclusion: There will be many that say they abide in Christ; however, the fruit of their lives will bear out the evidence. If they are fruitless, they are the 'tares' that will be separated out. A genuine believer will bear the fruit of conversion... Verse eight sums up the parable: if we do not bear fruit, we do not actually have eternal life; our abode is not really in Him, neither is His abode in us.

John 17:12

> NASB: "While I was with them, I was keeping them in Your name which You have given Me; and I guarded them and not one of them perished but the son of perdition, so that the Scripture would be fulfilled".

> KJV: "While I was with them in the world, I kept them in Thy name: those that thou gavest me I have kept, and none of them is lost, but the son of perdition; that the scripture might be fulfilled".

Context: Jesus is praying to His Father. In verse 11, He seems to be passing the mantle of responsibility of not losing any back to His Father. This prayer is specifically for the chosen apostles at this point. One of which was known to be the "son of perdition" – which is a figure of speech to describe one that is destined to perish. Later in verse 20, Jesus says this prayer is also for all believers.

Comments:
- Jesus demonstrated that not one of His disciples perished – except the one who was chosen in full knowledge and by design to do so – the son of perdition. Jesus was actively guarding and preserving these believers to remain in the faith. The word 'keeping' is an important verb meaning that *in the*

past and continuously Jesus was actively keeping them in the faith (in Thy name).

Summation: This verse provides assurance for our eternal security.

Further Explanation: Jesus takes an active role in guarding us once we are His.

Opposing View: The fact that Judas Iscariot, who was a chosen apostle, was *lost*, shows that we can be lost.

Conclusion: This is an isolated incident of someone being identified as lost by design. Based on what characterized Judas' life, it appears more reasonable that Judas was never really converted to Christ. In God's foreknowledge, Christ chose Judas fully knowing that Judas would be the one to betray Christ and therefore, aid in the fulfillment of God's plan of redemption. There would be no reason for a genuine believer today to lose salvation in order to help fulfill God's plan of redemption.

Romans 8:38-39

> NASB: "For I am convinced that neither death, nor life, nor angels, nor principalities, nor things present, nor things to come, no powers, nor height, nor depth, nor any other created thing, will be able to separate us from the love of God, which is in Christ Jesus".

> KJV: "For I am persuaded, that neither death, nor life, nor angels, nor principalities, nor powers, nor things present, nor things to come, nor height, nor depth, nor any other creature, shall be able to separate us from the love of God, which is in Christ Jesus our Lord".

Context: Paul is encouraging the believers and assuring them of the finished work of Christ. As he wraps up His discourse in chapter 8, he concludes by elaborating that none of these described can separate us from God's love for us in Christ Jesus.

Comments:
- The love of God for us is manifest by Christ in us. God is the one who justifies (v. 30). If He is for us, who can be against us (v.31)?
- The subject verses above are the answers to Paul's question in verse 35... who shall separate us from the love of Christ?

Summation: This verse provides assurance for our eternal security.

Further Explanation: The work of our justification is completed by God alone. Who has the power to undo what God has done? No created thing can undo His handy work in Paul's persuasion.

Opposing View: The argument is that, though no other created thing can separate us from God, we can by our freewill separate ourselves. However, this is an assumption that is not made in the text.

Conclusion: Why would a genuine believer want to separate himself from his maker? The only way a person would get to that state of mind is to be deceived by the enemy himself. Can the devil deceive us into thinking that we do not need Christ and therefore should denounce our faith in Him? If so, then in fact, what Paul tells us is not true. The devil is a created thing that would then have been successful at separating us from Christ. Does God grant us the most precious gift? – Salvation – then entrust the frailty of our thinking to maintain what He has freely given? Are we created things, more powerful than Christ who guards those who are His? May it never be!

Romans 13:11

> NASB: "Do this, knowing the time, that it is already the hour for you to awaken from sleep; for now salvation is nearer to us than when we believed".

KJV: "And that, knowing the time, that now it is high time to awake out of sleep; for now is our salvation nearer than when we believed".

Context: Paul is telling the believers that they need to be aware of the times and to live in such a manner as is pleasing to Christ. As the end is near, be found doing it right.

Comments:
- There was a point when these believers "first" believed – "when we believed". Believed is the Greek word *pisteuo* (Strong's #4100) which is that point in time when one puts his trust and confidence in Christ for salvation.
- "Believed" is past tense indicating an event took place in the past rather than one that is taking place in the present.
- Paul states that the fulfillment of their trust in Christ is growing nearer. The result of our placing trust in Christ is to be with Him eternally.

Summation: This verse provides assurance for our eternal salvation.

Further Explanation: This passage demonstrates that we are saved at a specific point in time – when we first believed. Salvation is not an ongoing, insecure process (although, our sanctification is ongoing).

Opposing View: N/A

Conclusion: This passage demonstrates that conversion to Christ takes place at a specific point in time. If we once believed (and bore fruit proving our conversion was genuine), then we can rest assured that we are His and the fulfillment of our trust in Him is drawing nearer.

1 Corinthians 3:12-15

NASB: "Now if any man builds on the foundation with gold, silver, precious stones, wood, hay, straw, each man's work will become evident; for the day will show it because it is to be revealed with fire, and the fire itself will test the quality of each man's work. If any man's work which he has built on it remains, he will receive a reward. If any man's work is burned up, he will suffer loss; but he himself will be saved, yet so as through fire".

KJV: "Now if any man build upon this foundation gold, silver, precious stones, wood, hay, stubble; Every man's work shall be made manifest: for the day shall declare it, because it shall be revealed by fire; and the fire shall try every man's work of what sort it is. If any man's work abide which he hath built thereupon, he shall receive a reward. If any man's work shall be burned, he shall suffer loss: but he himself shall be saved; yet so as by fire".

Context: Paul is explaining the value of making sure we spend our lives producing "lasting fruit" or "eternal works". Verse 8 explains that we receive a reward for laboring in the harvest. Verses 11 through 15 further the thought about the quality of work. Lasting fruit receives a reward; temporal or earthly fruit will be burned up – but the believer will still be saved.

Comments:
- This is the judgment of the saints, not a judgment to determine salvation as will be for the sinner, but a judgment of how we lived our lives on earth.

Summation: This verse provides assurance for our eternal security.

Further Explanation: The external fruit that we produce (or do not) in our lives is not what determines our salvation.

Opposing View: N/A

Conclusion: This passage is not a license to sin knowing that we are saved. Rather, it is an exhortation for the genuine believer to grow in Christ and live a fruitful life to receive a good reward in the last day. If we have works that will be burned up, we will still be saved, yet as through fire, according to Paul.

1 Corinthians 9:27

> NASB: "but I discipline my body and make it my slave, so that, after I have preached to others, I myself will not be disqualified".

> KJV: "But I keep under my body, and bring it into subjection; lest that by any means, when I have preached to others, I myself should be cast away".

Context: Paul is teaching the church that how they live their lives is important for the spreading of the gospel. He encourages them to stay focused on the eternal, imperishable prize.

Comments:
- Paul has had to address many behavior issues with the Corinthians. He is now encouraging them to maintain self-control knowing that others outside the faith are watching.
- The keyword is "disqualified" which is the Greek word *Adokimos* (Strong's #96). It means cast away, rejected, or reprobate. In context, it refers to being rejected by those Paul (or the others) are trying to win to Christ. Based on context, the term cannot mean to be "cast away" or "rejected" from salvation.
- It would be unfruitful to preach the holy life – a life of Christ-likeness – to others and yet not have self-control yourself. Those who witness such hypocrisy could then reject the message and the messenger.

Summation: *This verse is neither for nor against eternal security.*

Further Explanation: The passage speaks of being a good Christian witness so others will receive the message.

Opposing View: It would have to be said that Paul was concerned about being rejected by Christ if Paul did not discipline his body and make it his slave. The context does not support this argument.

Conclusion: Paul is showing by example how to be a good Christian witness – demonstrate a disciplined life that matches the message preached.

1 Corinthians 10:12

> NASB: "Therefore let him who thinks he stands take heed lest he fall".

> KJV: "Wherefore let him that thinketh he standeth take heed lest he fall".

Context: Paul uses the example of the Israelites in the wilderness. He shows how even though God was leading them, God was not pleased with most of them (v. 5) because of their sinful acts.

Comments:
- "Fall" is the Greek word *pipto* (Strong's #4098) meaning "to fall from a state of uprightness, i.e., to sin[19]".
- The warning here is for Christians to not take for granted the leading and provision of God in our lives as if He makes us immune from sinning – He does not.
- Verse 13 clears up any confusion about our position in Christ being secure… "God is faithful who will not allow you to be tempted beyond what you are able".

Summation: Verse 12 is neither for nor against eternal security. However, verse 13 offers assurance of God's work in keeping us from being tempted beyond our capacity to resist.

Further Explanation: Those who have the Spirit of the living God within them have an assurance that God will "not allow you to be tempted beyond what you are able".

Opposing View: This verse is used to elaborate on the concept that a Christian can "fall" from salvation. The context does not support this argument. The fact that the Children of Israel were physically killed for their sins and/or kept from the Promised Land does not mean that a Christian can lose salvation.

Conclusion: Even when temptations come, God makes sure we can resist. Further, we are not to be arrogant as Christians and think that we can stand without the grace of God.

1 Corinthians 15:2

> NASB: "by which also you are saved, if you hold fast the word which I preached to you, unless you believed in vain".

> KJV: "By which also ye are saved, if ye keep in memory what I preached unto you, unless ye have believed in vain".

Context: Paul has been addressing many issues, problems and concerns of the church in Corinth. Here in chapter 15 he is addressing the fact that some deny the resurrection. This calls into question the validity of their salvation.

Comments:
- Paul addresses a serious issue in that some are denying the resurrection. He states that to do so means their faith would have been in vain.

- To have genuine salvation, one must believe the correct gospel – that which Paul certainly preached, and not Paul only.
- Paul says he is making known to them that the gospel which he originally preached to them, which they received, which they now stand and are currently saved, is only a value to them if they, at the time he first preached and they first received, had believed all that he preached.
- Otherwise, they had at that point believed in vain.
- "Hold fast" is the Greek word *katecho* (Strong's #2722) means: "To have, hold fast, keep in memory, hold firmly[20]"

Summation: *This verse is neither for nor against eternal security.*

Further Explanation: Paul does not appear to be saying that these people were saved but then would no longer be saved if they discontinued believing the correct gospel. Rather, he seems to be saying that they are saved if they are currently demonstrating that they had first believed the correct gospel. Had they not accepted the resurrection, they would have been thinking they were saved, but that belief would be in vain.

Opposing View: On the surface, this passage seems to indicate that one can lose one's salvation if one does not stay in the faith. If one stops believing in the resurrection, then one is no longer saved. However, the key phrase is, "unless you believed in vain". This is past tense indicating that their believing was either correct or incorrect when they first believed.

Conclusion: Our conversion to Christ must be based on the correct gospel message which includes the resurrection. If we are not holding fast to that message, then we are holding fast to a gospel that cannot save us.

2 Corinthians 13:5

> NASB: "Test yourselves to see if you are in the faith; examine yourselves! Or, do you not recognize this about yourselves, that Jesus Christ is in you – unless indeed you fail the test"?

> KJV: "Examine yourselves, whether yet be in the faith; prove your own selves. Know ye not your own selves, how that Jesus Christ is in you, except ye be reprobates"?

Context: Paul is writing to a church that is having a large variety of problems with sin. He makes a strong statement for them to examine themselves to see if they are in the faith.

Comments:
- "Fail the test" (NASB) or "reprobates" (KJV) is the Greek word *adokimos* (Strong's #96) meaning "unapproved, unworthy, spurious, worthless, disapproved, rejected, cast away[21]".

Summation: This verse is neither for nor against eternal security.

Further Explanation: This passage is an encouragement to the believers that Christ is in them.

Opposing View: Paul seems to be saying that we should examine ourselves at times to see if we are 'still in the faith'. However, he does not tell these believers to test themselves to see if they are still in faith. He immediately reminds them, even encourages them, that Christ is in them. The only way that Christ could not be in them, he says, is if their self-examination were to prove that they did not have Christ. This would be if they had at first "believed in vain" (See 1 Cor 15:2 Pg 74).

Conclusion: Throughout Paul's letters, he addresses various sins running rampant in the church. He is now reminding the Corinthians that since Christ is in them, they need to behave appropriately (v. 7).

Galatians 5:4

> NASB: "You have been severed from Christ, you who are seeking to be justified by law; you have fallen from grace".

> KJV: "Christ is become of no effect unto you, whosoever of you are justified by the law; ye are fallen from grace".

Context: A group of people (v. 12) is trying to deceive the believers in Galatia. Paul is reminding the believers of the freedom they found in Christ. He also addresses those who have chosen to be justified by law rather than by Christ. Those who are trying to mislead the believers are preaching that one must be circumcised or in other words, work for their salvation. This infers that Christ is not enough.

Comments:
- The primary point being made is where the person's trust is placed. Is their trust placed in Christ alone by grace, or do they trust in the works of the law? It cannot be both.
- Paul has confidence that the true believers will remain steadfast. He also points out there are some who are trying to deceive them. These deceivers will be cut-off. These chose the law over Christ.
- The King James Version has a better, more accurate rendering of the text in verse 2, "…if ye be circumcised" – those who claim to be circumcised – those who in essence are justified by the law.
- In verse 4, "…you are justified by the law" rather than "seeking to be" as if the believer is seeking a further justification.
- "Severed from Christ" is better translated in the King James Version, "Christ is become of no effect unto you…" These are the deceivers who have chosen the wrong path – that of law rather than grace.

- "Fallen from grace" is not meaning losing one's salvation. The ones who are justified by law have fallen from grace – that is, they have kept themselves away from the path of grace.

Summation: This verse is neither for nor against eternal security.

Further Explanation: Those who choose to be justified by law do not receive the benefit of the saving of God.

Opposing View: This view believes that genuine believers who decide, after being born-again, that they will trust in the law rather than grace alone. Therefore, they have been severed from Christ. After all, one can only be severed from what one is first attached to. However, this is a presupposition that these are genuine believers who have been severed or fallen from grace. Verse 4 specifically points to the people in verse 12 who are "justified by law" and confusing the believers. Paul is stating that the ones who are justified by law – the unbelievers – have caused themselves to be alienated from Christ, to have kept themselves away from grace. He is exhorting the genuine believers not to be swayed by these deceivers.

Conclusion: This verse indirectly gives assurance of Christ's grace that frees us from the law. It also informs us how to live right for Christ.

Ephesians 1:13-14

> NASB: "In Him, you also, after listening to the message of truth, the gospel of your salvation – having also believed, you were sealed in Him with the Holy Spirit of promise, who is given as a pledge of our inheritance, with a view to the redemption of God's own possession, to the praise of His glory".

> KJV: "In whom ye also trusted, after that ye heard the word of truth, the gospel of your salvation: in whom also after that ye believed, ye were sealed with that Holy Spirit of promise,

which is the earnest of our inheritance until the redemption of the purchased possession, unto the praise of his glory".

Context: Paul is reassuring those in Ephesus – the faithful saints – that Christ is the one who chose them and predestined them to salvation. As a down payment or sign of earnest on the contract to purchase them, they were sealed with the Holy Spirit. Those who believed were then sealed by God.

Comments:
- Who is able to break the Kings' seal? This seal is the promise that we will see the fulfillment of our redemption.
- Christ purchased us by His blood, and when we believe, He gives us the earnest or down payment on that purchase.
- The final offer is consummated upon the redemption of our bodies in the resurrection.

Summation: This verse provides assurance for our eternal security.

Further Explanation: When we receive the seal of the Holy Spirit living in our hearts, we are guaranteed our redemption and final home in heaven.

Opposing View: This view says that the Holy Spirit is given only as a pledge. Therefore, we must maintain our part in order to make the contract valid on the last day. If we fall away, we lose the Holy Spirit. We are no longer sealed. However, once a believer is sealed, the believers' fate is set. The seal is that "God knows who are His" and He gives His spirit to them. Nothing can change that.

Conclusion: When we are sealed by God, we are His forever.

Ephesians 4:30

NASB: "And do not grieve the Holy Spirit of God, by whom you were sealed for the day of redemption".

> KJV: "And grieve not the holy spirit of God, whereby ye are sealed unto the day of redemption".

Context: The entirety of chapter four is discussing Christian conduct. We are told to "walk in a manner worthy of the calling" (v. 1) and "walk no longer as the Gentiles" (v. 17). We are to live in such a way as to "not grieve [or offend] the Holy Spirit of God" (v. 30).

Comments:
- The main point of this passage is to live in such a manner as to not offend the Spirit of God. There is no reference to that offense leading to a loss of salvation.
- The phrase "sealed for the day of redemption" is the key phrase.
- "Sealed" is the Greek word *aphragizo* (Strong's #4972) which means "respecting God, who by the gift of the Holy Spirit indicates who are his[22]".
- The question is whether the seal is permanent or can be broken.
- "Redemption" is the Greek word *apolutrosis* (Strong's #629) which means "the recalling of captives (sinners) from captivity (sin) through the payment of a ransom for them, i.e., Christ's death[23]".
- The entire phrase is further defined, "the last day, when consummate liberation is experienced from the sin still lingering even in the regenerate, and from all the ills and troubles of this life[24]".
- What is the deal of God? "Nevertheless, the firm foundation of God stands, having this seal, 'the Lord knows those who are His'" (2 Tim 2:19, emphasis added).

Summation: This verse provides assurance for our eternal security.

Further Explanation: Though we may waiver at times about our salvation, we have this seal "…the Lord knows those who are His".

Opposing View: Though we are sealed, it is not a guarantee that the deal cannot be broken. Another view could be that the seal is no more than a "mark" or "identification" that exits while someone is saved. If one loses salvation, one no longer bears the seal. However, even if the seal could be broken, the author is not saying that grieving the Holy Spirit will or can break the seal.

Conclusion: When we are saved, we are sealed and remain in that condition until the 'day of redemption'.

Philippians 1:6

> NASB: "For I am confident of this very thing, that He who began a good work in you will perfect it until the day of Christ Jesus".

> KJV: "Being confident of this very thing, that he which hath begun a good work in you will perform it until the day of Jesus Christ".

Context: Paul is writing the believers in Philippi. He has seen the fruit they are bearing in their faith. He commands them and states his confidence in the fact that it is, has been, and will be Christ working in them.

Comments:
- The day of the Lord is referring to the Lord's second coming. Perfect it or (perform it) is the Greek word *epiteleo* (Strong's #2005) meaning "to finish, complete, perfect, to perform to accomplish[25]".

Summation: This verse provides assurance for our eternal security.

Further Explanation: Because it is Christ who begins the work in us, it will be Him who also completes it.

Opposing View: n/a

Conclusion: Though we may stumble, Christ will not let us fall – He will finish what He started in us.

Philippians 2:12-13

> NASB: "So then, my beloved, just as you have always obeyed, not as in my presence only, but now much more in my absence, work out your salvation with fear and trembling; for it is God who is at work in you, both to will and to work for His good pleasure".

> KJV: "Wherefore, my beloved, as ye have always obeyed, not as in my presence only, but now much more in my absence, work out your salvation with fear and trembling. For it is God which worketh in you both to will and to do of his good pleasure".

Context: The author instructs the recipients to remain humble in their fellowship with one another. He then uses Christ as an example of humility. The subject verse is the author's command summarizing the previous exhortations.

Comments:
- "Fear and trembling" is a common phrase of that era (See Strong's #5156). According to Thayer's, it means "with fear and trembling, used to describe the anxiety of one who distrusts his ability completely to meet all requirements, but religiously does his utmost to fulfill his duty[26]".
- "Work out" is the Greek word *katergazomai* (Strong's #2716). Its use in this text is the Present Middle Imperative. Present tense shows that the action is continuous. The middle voice indicates that the subject initiates the action and also participates in the results of the action. The imperative mood is a demand on the will of the reader to obey the command.

Summation: This verse is neither for nor against eternal security.

Further Explanation: The term "work out" being in the middle voice means that the reader is to initiate the action. Since we know that humankind cannot initiate our eternal salvation, the author cannot be telling us that we are to do so. Rather, the author in verse 12 is commending the recipients for obeying Christ. He explains that we are responsible for taking the initiative to "perform deeds appropriate to repentance" (Acts 26:20). With fear and trembling balances our works in that we are told to not trust in our ability to fulfill our obligation to perform good works. The paradox is that we are told to do good works, but yet, in verse 13, we are told that it is actually God who is at work in us.

Opposing View: "Work out" must mean we are to do good works in order to keep our salvation. However, this interpretation goes against the grammatical structure of the passage. Furthermore, if salvation is a gift from God that we cannot earn through good works, how is it that we must do good works after we are saved to "earn" the right to keep the gift?

Conclusion: We do have a responsibility to live godly lives; however, God is the One who empowers us to do so.

Colossians 1:22-23

> NASB: "Yet He has now reconciled you in His fleshly body through death, in order to present you before Him holy and blameless and beyond reproach, if indeed you continue in the faith firmly established and steadfast, and not moved away from the hope of the gospel that you have heard, which has proclaimed in all creation under heaven, and of which I, Paul, was made a minister".

> KJV: "yet now hath he reconciled in the body of his flesh through death, to present you holy and unblameable and unreproveable in his sight: if yet continue in the faith grounded and settled, and be not moved away from the hope of the

gospel, which ye have heard, and which was preached to every creature which is under heave; whereof I Paul am made a minister".

Context: Paul is praising the church for their steadfast faith. He is reminding them of whom they believe.

Comments:
- Paul states emphatically that Christ has reconciled the believers to Himself. However, he adds what seems to be a conditional statement – if indeed you continue in the faith. So, it seems that we are reconciled only if we "continue" in the faith.
- "Continue" is the Greek word *epimeno* (Strong's #1961). It simply means *to remain on, to continue long*, i.e., to continue in the faith.
- "Reconciled" in verse 22 is the Greek word *apokatallasso* (Strong's #604) meaning to "reconcile completely[27]". It refers to the finished work of reconciling the unbeliever to God. It is in the Aorist Active Indicative verb tense which refers to a past time.
- "Established" is the Greek word *themelioo* (Strong's #2311) simply meaning to *lay a foundation, to be grounded, to be founded*. It is in the Perfect Passive Participle that indicates it is an action that took place in the past but has continuing results.
- "If indeed" is the Greek word *eige* (Strong's #1489) which also means "seeing that, unless otherwise[28]".

Summation: This verse provides assurance for our eternal security.

Further Explanation: This verse identifies a genuine believer. It does not say a genuine believer can be "un-reconciled" if the believer does not continue in the faith. Paul is stating that one who has been in the past reconciled is identified by "continuing in the faith". One who does not continue in the faith us, as John states it, "not really of us".

Opposing View: One is only reconciled if one continues in the faith. However, the act of reconciliation takes place at a specific point in time. The passage says, "has now reconciled", not "will continue to reconcile".

Conclusion: Not everyone who professes to be Christian is truly reconciled to Christ. Those who have been reconciled will bear the fruit. Those who have not will eventually grow weary of religion and thus, not continue in the faith.

2 Thessalonians 2:3

> NASB: "Let no one in any way deceive you, for it will not come unless the apostasy comes first, and the man of lawlessness is revealed, the son of destruction".

> KJV: "Let no many deceive you by any means: for that day shall not come, except there come a falling away first, and that man of sin be revealed, the son of perdition"

Context: To counteract some false teachers claiming the second coming has happened, Paul explains to the brethren what to watch for – signs of the false coming.

Comments:
- Paul is encouraging the brethren to not be shaken by the false teachings.
- Paul explains in verses 10 through 12 that the ones who will be deceived are those who chose not to believe in the saving truth – the unbelievers.
- In fact, God will at the time of his coming, "send upon them a deluding influence so that they will believe what is false" (v. 11). This is because they did not believe.
- Paul then reassures the brethren of their position in Christ (v. 13-14). He states, "because God has chosen you from the beginning for salvation… (v. 13) and they were called to "gain the glory of our Lord Jesus Christ" (v. 14). He prays for their

comfort and strengthened hearts through the Lord who has given us "eternal comfort and good hope by grace" (v. 16).

- The "apostasy" is further described as "the rebellion":
    - o "The rebellion", a Hellenistic formation, corresponding to classical [Apostasia], denotes either political rebellion (as in Josephus, vita 43, of the Jewish revolt against Rome) or religious defection (as in Acts 21:21, of abandonment of Moses' law). Since the reference here is to a world-wide rebellion against divine authority at the end of the age, the ideas of political revolt and religious apostasy are combined[29]".
    - o It appears more probable from the context that a general abandonment of the basis of civil order is envisaged. This is not only rebellion against the law of Moses; it is a large-scale revolt against public order, and since public order is maintained by the 'governing authorities' who 'have been instituted by God', any assault on it is an assault on a divine ordinance (Rom 13:1,2). It is, in fact, the whole concept of divine authority over the world that is set at defiance in 'the rebellion' par excellance[30]".

Summation: This verse is neither for nor against eternal security.

Further Explanation: The verse simply explains the signs of the second coming.

Opposing View: Some argue that this passage shows many believers will fall away in the great apostasy. However, this passage does not address believers as a whole nor does it address individuals. Verses 10 through 12 do describe those who will be known as apostate. They will be the unbelievers; those who chose not to accept Christ.

Conclusion: The apostasy described in this letter is a time when God will send a "deluding influence" (v. 11) on the population of unbelievers because they already chose not to believe. Genuine believers will not be found "apostate" during the time described when the man of lawlessness appears.

1 Timothy 1:19-20

> NASB: "…keeping faith and a good conscience, which some have rejected and suffered shipwreck in regard to their faith. Among these are Hymenaeus and Alexander, whom I have delivered unto Satan that they may learn not to blaspheme".

> KJV: "Holding faith, and a good conscience; which some having put away concerning faith have made shipwreck: Of whom is Hymenaeus and Alexander; whom I have delivered unto Satan, that they may learn not to blaspheme."

Context: Paul is instructing Timothy throughout his two letters to guard against false teachers. He appears to name at least two of them in this letter. He adds Philetus to the list in his second letter. He also references Alexander the coppersmith in 2 Timothy 4:14 as one who vigorously opposes the apostles teaching. This may well be the same Alexander in this passage.

Comments:
- It seems difficult to consider Hymenaeus and Alexander genuine believers who subsequently "rejected" the faith.
- Paul seems to describe "certain men" (1 Tim 1\:3) as teaching strange or other doctrines. They are said to be "straying" (v. 6). These certain men are "liars" and "seared in conscience" (2.2). They are: conceited, understand nothing, have a morbid interest in controversial questions (v. 4), men of "depraved mind", "deprived of the truth", and suppose godliness is a means of great gain (v. 6). They profess "false knowledge" and have gone astray from the truth" (v. 21).
- Hymenaeus and Alexander are pointed out as examples of the type of men to stay away from (1 Tim 1:20).

- Paul says he will hand these to Satan to be taught to not blaspheme.
- It appears that these "certain men" are not "true children of the faith" as Paul refers to Timothy (1:2).

Summation: This verse is neither for nor against eternal security.

Further Explanation: Based on the overall context of the letter to Timothy, these men are being identified as false teachers who are to be taught a lesson.

Opposing View: Because the verse says that Hymenaeus and Alexander rejected… in regard to their faith, it proves that they had faith then rejected it. However, the verse does not say they had saving faith. If, however, they did have saving faith, the verse also does not say that they lost their salvation. At best, if these men are genuine believers, they will be taught a hard lesson about teaching false doctrine. Paul will hand them over to Satan like he did to the man in 1 Corinthians 5. The lesson is not to "blaspheme" which Thayer's defines in this context as, "speak reproachfully, rail at, revile, calumnite[31]".

Conclusion: Context demonstrates that these men are false teachers. They have blasphemed – rejected Christ. Paul is identifying them as a source of trouble in the church. They need to be dealt with.

1 Timothy 4:1

> NASB: "But the Spirit explicitly says that in latter times some will fall away from the faith, paying attention to deceitful spirits and doctrines of demons".

> KJV: "Now the Spirit speaketh expressly, that in the latter times some shall depart from the faith, giving heed to seducing spirits, and doctrines of devils".

Context: Paul opens this letter to Timothy regarding men apparently in the congregation that are professing a false knowledge and teaching these falsehoods. These men in chapter 1, verse 6 and in chapter 6, verse 21 have strayed away from or left the faith. They are teachers of the law. Paul continues to elaborate on the needs and teachings of these men.

Comments:
- The term "falling away from the faith" does not state "losing the benefits of eternal salvation".
- The Greek word for faith is the noun *pritis* (Strong's #4101). In this context it is used to describe the "Christian religion". These men Paul refers to are associated with or seeking after the Christian religion. However, they are apparently turning aside to false teachings and legalism.

Summation: This verse is neither for nor against eternal security.

Further Explanation:

Opposing View: Some might argue that to "fall away" from the faith would mean one had to first be "in" the faith and by "in the faith" mean that one "has" saving faith. Then, at some uncertain point, that person, either consciously or unconsciously, falls out of union with that saving faith. Therefore, they have "lost" their salvation. By paying attention to or by being deceived by deceitful spirits and wrong doctrines, one can lose salvation. This view again presupposes that we cannot earn our salvation but have to work meritoriously to keep it. In context, however, Paul never indicates that these people ever had salvation, though they are among the congregation. Further, these people are described throughout the letter as teaching false doctrines. Paul names Hymenaeus and Alexander as being among this group (1:20). These men are blasphemers and oppose Paul's teaching (2 Tim 2:17, 4:14).

Conclusion: This passage further describes the apostasy of the latter times. (See What if I become apostate, Pg 29).

1 Timothy 4:16

> NASB: "Pay close attention to yourself and to your teaching; persevere in these things, for as you do this you will ensure salvation both for yourself and for those who hear you.

> KJV: "Take heed unto thyself, and unto the doctrine; continue in them; for in doing this thou shalt both save thyself and them that hear thee".

Context: Paul is exhorting Timothy to be a good example of a believer, both in action and in teaching. He warns that some will be deceived by false teachers and fall away from the faith.

Comments:
- The word "salvation" or "saved" is the Greek word *sozo* (Strong's #4982) meaning, to save. It is a verb as more correctly translated in the King James Version as opposed to the noun *soteria* as described in the NASB version. The verb is in the Future Active Indicative form meaning it is a continuous action in the future as initiated by the subject of the action. In other words, it is a statement of fact.
- The Interlinear Greek-English Bible translates the verb as "deliver[32]". Zodhiates explains it as "the present experience of God's power to deliver from the bondage of sin; human agency in this[33]".

Summation: This verse is neither for nor against eternal security.

Further Explanation: Rather than being a passage regarding eternal security, this passage teaches how believers are to live.

Opposing View: This view says that if we persevere, we will keep our salvation. If we do not, we will lose it. However, Paul is addressing Timothy's character and teaching. Timothy will then ensure the sanctification process of salvation will continue in him and in others. Since the active verb, *sozo*, means that the subject of the verb,

Timothy, initiates the action, we conclude that the action is godly living "since it holds promise for the present life and also for the life to come" (v. 8). Timothy has to initiate this godly lifestyle; he cannot initiate, however, his salvation.

Conclusion: The verb usage of the word that is translated salvation is the key to understanding this passage. Since humankind cannot initiate salvation, and since salvation is a process that includes, conversion, sanctification, and glorification, this verb is not referring to our conversions. Rather, it refers to the sanctification process of our salvation.

2 Timothy 1:12

> NASB: "For this reason I also suffer these things, but I am not ashamed; for I know whom I have believed and am convinced that He is able to guard what I have entrusted to Him until that day".

> KJV: "For which cause I also suffer these things; nevertheless I am not ashamed: for I know whom I have believed, and am persuaded that he is able to keep that which I have committed unto him against that day".

Context: Paul is exhorting Timothy. Paul comments on Timothy's faith and Christ's work in bringing salvation. He then explains why he is willing to suffer and is not ashamed. He knows whom he has believed and trusts Him with that belief and his very life.
Comments:
- Paul has entrusted his soul to Christ. Therefore, he is confident that he can trust Christ to guard it until that day.

Summation: This verse provides assurance for our eternal security.

Further Explanation: We can as well place our trust in Christ to guard us until that day. Our salvation is not up to us to obtain or maintain.

Opposing View: It might be thought that we must continue to trust Christ. If we stop trusting Him, we can lose our salvation. However, we notice that Paul said, "I know whom I *have* believed" and "what I *have* entrusted". This refers to him placing his belief and trust in Christ at some point in the past. He does not say, "I know whom I am believing" or "what I am entrusting" – though, we can be confident from what we have in Scripture that Paul did continue to trust and believe in Christ without wavering.

Conclusion: Once we have placed our trust in Christ, He will guard us until we are finally with Him.

2 Timothy 2:11-13

> NASB: "It is a trustworthy statement: for if we died with him, we will also live with Him; if we endure, we will also reign with Him; if we deny Him, He will also deny us; if we are faithless, He remains faithful, for He cannot deny Himself".

> KJV: "It is a faithful saying: for if we be dead with him, we shall also live with him; if we suffer, we shall also reign with him; if we deny him, he will also deny us; if we believe not, yet he abideth faithful; he cannot deny himself".

Context: Paul is encouraging Timothy to suffer for the gospel like he is suffering. In verse ten he explains that he is willing to suffer for those who still need to receive salvation. He then moves right into a very simple explanation of the gospel.

Comments:
- The simplicity of the Gospel is laid out in these verses like a poem:
  - Those who die with Christ, receive eternal life – salvation.
  - Those believers who endure hardships for Him also will reign with Him – an additional honor or reward.

- o Those who deny Christ are in turn, rejected by Him – unbelievers.
- o Even though some will not believe, Christ does not change – He remains faithful and it cannot be said that He is unjust.
- "We" in these verses does not automatically apply to believers only. Paul lays the groundwork for this statement in verse ten where he is referring to unbelievers.
- The "we" in the first two stanzas of verse 11 refer to believers. The "we" in the last two stanzas refer to unbelievers.
- The "we" in the third line, "if we deny Him…" cannot refer to believers denying Christ and losing salvation otherwise, Peter would have lost his salvation when He denied Christ three times. (Peter could not have been born-again, again – and again, etc.).
- The last line, "if we are faithless" is referring to unbelievers. Though these have no faith, Christ remains the same and everything He stands for remains the same. If one wants to interpret the "faithless" as backslidden believers, Christ still remains the same. He does not waiver.
- Further, the first line provides tremendous assurance: if we died with Him, we will live with Him.

Summation: This verse provides assurance our eternal security.

Further Explanation: We are assured that if we died with Him, we will also live with Him.

Opposing View: This view states that if a believer denies Christ, then Christ will deny the believer eternal life. Because Paul is saying "we", he must mean the believers. However, throughout Paul's writings, he includes false teachers and false prophets n his addressing the "brethren". His letters are written to the congregations in general knowing that not everyone in the congregation is a genuine believer. Paul addresses vessels of honor and of dishonor in verse 20. He explains his hope that unbelievers would become saved in verse 25 and 26.

<u>Conclusion</u>: If we died (in the past) with Christ, we will live (forever) with Him.

2 Timothy 2:18

> NASB: "Men who have gone astray from the truth saying that the resurrection has already taken place, and they upset the faith of some".

> KJV: "Who concerning the truth have erred, saying that the resurrection is past already; and overthrow the faith of some".

<u>Context</u>: Paul is referring to Hymenaeus and Philetus. There are causing strive and injuring the faith of some. Paul exhorts Timothy to handle accurately the truth. He is to avoid these worldly debates that are ungodly. These are the opposing "arguments of what is falsely called 'knowledge'". (1 Tim 6:20)

<u>Comments</u>:
- Hymenaeus is described in Timothy's first letter as a blasphemer (1 Tim 1:20). He may also be of those in 1 Tim 6:20-12 who was involved in "worldly and empty chatter and the opposing arguments of what is falsely called 'knowledge' – which some have professed and thus gone astray from the faith".
- This useless wrangling about words which ruins people's faith (2 Tim 2:14) is considered "worldly and empty chatter" (v. 16) and leads to further ungodliness. In fact, this kind of talk is like a cancer that spreads (v. 17).
- Apparently these men had a worldly philosophy they were introducing. They did not have the truth.
- The King James Version says they "erred" concerning the truth.
- Paul instructs Timothy to "pursue righteousness… with those who call on the Lord from a pure heart" (v. 22) indicating that some are calling on the name of the Lord out of a wicked or

impure heart. These are the ones who are "in opposition" (v. 25) that Timothy needs to gently correct so that maybe they will be granted "repentance leading to the knowledge of the truth, and that they may come to their senses and escape from the snare of the devil, having been held captive by him to do his will" (v. 25-26). They are unsaved men still in the captivity of their father, the devil. They are the ones in chapter three, verse 5 that have a "form of godliness"… "always learning but never able to come to the knowledge of the truth" (v. 7).

Summation: This verse is neither for nor against eternal security.

Further Explanation:

Opposing View: This argument hangs on the term "gone astray". It places Hymenaues and Philetus in the statue of genuine believers who have departed the faith. It is obvious, however, as noted in the above comments, that these men were not believers. Rather, they were a group that had only a form of religion but no relationship with Christ. However, even if they could somehow be considered brothers in Christ, there are nothing in this passage or group of passages that would lead one to believer with integrity that "gone away" means to become "unsaved".

Conclusion: This passage is a warning against false teachers and an exhortation to believers to be grounded in the Word of God.

2 Timothy 2:19

NASB: "Nevertheless, the firm foundation of God stands, having this seal, 'the Lord knows those who are His', and 'everyone who names the name of the Lord is to abstain from wickedness'".

KVJ: "Nevertheless the foundation of God standeth sure, having this seal, the Lord knoweth them that are his. And, let everyone that nameth the name of Christ depart from iniquity".

<u>Context</u>: Paul just sums up a discourse on the dissension that Hymenaeus and Philetus were causing. They were said to have "gone astray" – teaching false doctrine that the resurrection had already taken place. He then defines the firm foundation of God which has a seal that "the Lord knows those who are His", as opposed to Hymenaeus and Philetus who are obviously not.

<u>Comments</u>:
- We can be certain of this very foundation upon which our faith rests: the Lord knows those who are His!
- The Greek word for seal is *sphragis* (Strong's #4973) meaning: "A signet (as fencing in or protecting from misappropriation); by implication the stamp impressed (as a mark of privacy, or genuineness), literally or figuratively: seal[34]".
- Thayer's further defines seal to mean: "The inscription or impression made by a seal: Rev 9:4 (the name of God and Christ stamped upon their foreheads must be meant here, as is evident from Rev 14:1; 2 Tim 2:19)[35]".

<u>Summation</u>: *This verse provides assurance for our eternal security.*

<u>Further Explanation</u>: Genuine believers bear the seal of God – that He knows us. The emphasis is that He knows the ones who *are now* His, not the ones who *will be* His if they make it.

<u>Opposing View</u>: n/a
<u>Conclusion</u>: We have great confidence knowing that God knows His own and we are sealed in that knowledge.

2 Timothy 4:18

> NASB: "The Lord will rescue me from every evil deed, and will bring me safely to His heavenly kingdom; to Him be the glory forever and ever. Amen".

KJV: "And the Lord shall deliver me from every evil work, and will preserve me unto his heavenly kingdom: to whom be glory forever and ever. Amen".

Context: Paul's demise is eminent. Many have left him. Some have harmed him. He is in the midst of heavenly warfare. Paul is keenly aware of the battle. He makes the above statement with confidence.

Comments: n/a

Summation: *This verse provides assurance for our eternal security.*

Further Explanation: Paul demonstrates his confidence that the Lord will not only rescue him from all sorts of evil, but that He will bring Paul to his heavenly home at the appropriate time.

Opposing View: n/a

Conclusion: We can have the same confidence knowing that Christ will protect us and in time bring us home.

Titus 3:5

> NASB: "He saved us, not on the bases of deeds which we have done in righteousness, but according to His mercy, by the washing of regeneration and renewing by the Holy Spirit".

> KJV: "Not by works of righteousness which we have done, but according to his mercy he saved us, by the washing of regeneration, and renewing of the Holy Ghost".

Context: Paul is reminding Titus that we did nothing to merit God saving us. It was His kindness and mercy. Yet, we should do good works after the fact because they are profitable and good and render us faithful.

Comments:
- The emphasis is on the fact that Christ saved us by His mercy alone. We producing good works should then evidence His salvation.

Summation: This verse is neither for not against eternal security.

Further Explanation: This verse describes salvation by grace.

Opposing View: n/a

Conclusion: Salvation is the free gift of God not based on our works. How then can our works be meritorious toward keeping our salvation?

Hebrews 2:1-3

> NASB: "For this reason we must pay much closer attention to what we have heard, so that we not drift away from it. For if the word spoken through angels proved unalterable, and every transgression and disobedience received a just penalty, how will we escape if we neglect so great a salvation?"

KJV: "Therefore we ought to give the more earnest heed to the things which we have heard, lest at any time we should let them slip. For if the word spoken by angels was steadfast, and every transgression and disobedience received a just recompense of reward; how shall we escape, if we neglect so great salvation?"

Context: Hebrews seems to be written to the Jews by someone very familiar with the Law and Jewish ceremonial rites. The author is contrasting the old covenant with the new. Under the Old Testament, the follower must have faith and make an annual sacrifice for sin. Under the New Testament, the follower accepts by Faith Christ's once-for-all, eternal sacrifice for sin. Chapter two is a continuation of chapter one. In chapter one, the author gives a dissertation as to who Christ is. This is the reason (as chapter two opens) why the Jews need to pay close attention and not "drift away" from or "neglect" it.

Comments:
- The Greek word for "neglect" is *ameleo* (Strong's #272) meaning "to make light of, neglect, be negligent, not regard[36]". Thayer's defines it as "not caring for what had just been said [A.V. They made light of it][37]".
- The usage of *ameleo* is in the aorist participle expressing a "simple action, as opposed to the continuous action of the present participle[38]".
- The Greek word for "drift away" is *pararrhueo* (Strong's #3901) meaning to "carelessly pass – let slip[39]".
- Thayer's: "Lest we be carried past, pass by, [R.V. drift away from them] (missing the thing), if, lest the salvation which the things heard show us how to obtain, slip away from us[40]".

Summation: This verse is neither for nor against eternal security.

Further Explanation: This verse stresses the importance for the Jews (and everyone else) not to miss who Christ is and the great salvation He offers.

Opposing View: This view says that those who "drift away" and "neglect" their salvation will receive a just penalty – which is said to be eternal damnation. However, as indicated in the comments, this verse is not referring to genuine believers who lose their salvation. One also has to read into the "just penalty" to make it mean eternal damnation.

Conclusion: When the Gospel is presented to us, we are wise to receive it as the truth and embrace Christ as Lord and Savior. We should not "miss" this truth.

Hebrews 3:12

> NASB: "Take care, brethren, lest there should be in any one of you an evil, unbelieving heart, in falling away from the living God".

> KJV: "Take heed, brethren, lest there be in any of you an evil heart of unbelief, in departing from the living God".

Context: This verse is the beginning of an exhortation not to be like the children of Israel that Moses led out of Egypt (v. 16). They did not enter God's "rest" because of unbelief.

Comments:
- The keyword in this section is "rest". When do we enter His rest?
- It would appear that "enter His rest" (4:10) is to have "rested from his works" (v. 10).
- It appears that those who "have believed" (at a certain point in the past) (4:3), do at that time "enter the rest" (4:3).
- The Israelites that came out Egypt did not enter God's rest. They knew about it because they had the good news preached to them (4:1). However, though they knew of the rest, they did not have faith, so the word was unprofitable (4:2). They did not enter the rest (at any time) because of their unbelief (3:19).

- A couple phrases need to be addressed: chapter 3:6 "if we hold fast… until the end"; verse 12, "in falling away from the living God", and verse 14, "if we hold fast… until the end". None of these statements clearly indicate that it is a genuine believer – one who has already entered Christ's rest – that is subject to losing their salvation. These statements appear to be more like the admonition Paul gave to the Corinthians to examine themselves to see if "you are in the faith" (2 Cor 13\:5).
- John describes those who fall away or do not hold firm until the end when he states, 'they went out from us, but they were not really of us; for if they had been of us, they would have remained with us…" (1 John 2:19).
- Just because the author addresses the members of the congregation as "holy brethren, partakers of the heavenly calling" (3:1), does not mean that some might not be deceived about their salvation. The exhortation is to examine themselves – not to see if they have lost their salvation, but to make certain that their conversion was in the first place genuine.

Summation: *This verse is neither for nor against eternal security.*

Further Explanation: This is an exhortation to validate our salvation. Do we have the marks of genuine believers?

Opposing View: This passage shows that "brethren" can find themselves with an evil, unbelieving heart fallen away from God. However, as noted in the comments, "brethren" is used often to address mixed congregations. Not everyone in the congregation has had a genuine conversion.

Conclusion: It is wise to look at ourselves in the mirror and make sure that we are not deceiving ourselves about having a relationship with Christ. If we are His, we will show evidence of growth in our lives.

Hebrews 6:4-6

> NASB: "For in the case of those who have once been enlightened and have tasted of the heavenly gift and have been made partakers of the Holy Spirit, and have tasted the good word of God and the powers of the age to come, and then have fallen away, it is impossible to renew them again to repentance, since they again crucify to themselves the Son of God and put Him to open shame".

> KJV: "For it is impossible for those who were once enlightened, and have tasted of the heavenly gift, and were made partakers of the Holy Ghost, and have tasted the good word of God, and the powers of the world to come, if they shall fall away, to renew them again unto repentance; seeing they crucify themselves the Son of God afresh, and put him to open shame".

Context: The writer is explaining how to deal with sin in the life of a believer. Christ is the final sacrifice. Once the foundation of repentance from dead works and faith in God is laid in a person, it is no longer necessary to repeat that process as in the former days of annual sacrifices. In fact, it is impossible to do so. Christ's finished work is final. The author goes on to explain how to live and bear fruit in such a way as to receive the promises (note the plural form) of God.

Comments:
- The term "fall away" in this passage is the Greek word *parapipto* (Strong's #3895) which means to fall down, inadvertently. It is different from *parabaino* (Strong's #3845) which is to willfully sin or transgress. The passage clearly refers to a believer who stumbles into sin. It is not necessary to get born-again, again. In fact, it is impossible. The passage is not suggesting that to fall away means to lose salvation. It is a reminder that we can get back up and life the holy life. We should be mindful of our action to receive a blessing from God

and not have our works burned in the fire at the judgment of saints.

Summation: This verse provides assurance for our eternal security.

Further Explanation: This passage provides tremendous security for a genuine believer. Under the Old Testament sacrifice system, sin needed to be atoned for annually. In Christ, He completed our atonement once for all.

Opposing View: Those who have fallen away cannot be renewed to repentance. Therefore, they are now lost and eternally separated from Christ. They cannot be born-again, again. However, the context of the chapter and the entire book of Hebrews, demonstrates that Christ is sufficient as the final sacrifice for our sins allowing us to enter into His rest. We simply do not need to have another sacrifice each year – we cannot.

Conclusion: We have tremendous security knowing that our sins are atoned for once-for-all by Christ. Once we enter His rest, we do not need to look for another sacrifice.

Hebrews 10:14

> NASB: "For by one offering He has perfected for all time those who are sanctified".

> KJV: "For by one offering he hath perfected for ever them that are sanctified".

Context: The author is explaining the difference between the blood sacrifice of bulls and goats under the old covenant to the one-time sacrifice of Christ's blood under the new covenant.

Comments:
- The verse explains that the one-time offering by Christ is sufficient to perfect – or make to be right standing – those who are believers.
- Under the Old Covenant, those who sinned had to make a new offering each year. Under the New Covenant, the acceptance of the one-time offering of Christ is sufficient for all present and future sins of the believer. Christ does not have to make a sacrifice each year.
- "Perfected" is the Greek word *teleioo* (Strong's #5048) meaning "to perfect, to complete, to finish[41]". This is in the Perfect Indicative verb tense that means it happened, for certain, sometime in the past but its results continue into the future.
- What Christ did through His blood sacrifice replaces the need for ongoing blood sacrifices of bulls or goats.

Summation: *This verse provides assurance for our eternal security.*

Further Explanation: We take comfort knowing that Christ perfected us – for all time – with His atonement. We no longer need to bring sacrifices for our sins.

Opposing View: The term "sanctified" is more literally translated "being sanctified" which may then indicate that if someone ceases to continue "being sanctified", then Christ's offering is no longer applied. However, it is Christ's atonement that causes us to be in right standing with Him – justified. Sanctification is the ongoing, lifelong work that transforms the genuine believer into the image of Christ. Though we take some responsibility in the sanctification process, Christ initiates it and brings us back on track to complete it.

Conclusion: Christ's work of atonement is enough to bring us into right standing with Him, once for all.

Hebrews 10:26

> NASB: "For if we go on sinning willfully after receiving the knowledge of the truth, there no longer remains a sacrifice for sins".

> KJV: "For if we sin willfully after that we have received the knowledge of the truth, there remainteth no more sacrifice for sin".

Context: The entirety of chapter 10 appears to be written to those who are believers. It describes what the life of a true believe should look like. The author seems to be encouraging them in their faith.

Comments:
- To understand this verse (and others) in context, a careful examination of the entire chapter is necessary.
- The sacrifice is in reference to the annual sacrifices of bulls and goats (v. 4).
- Those sacrifices were not enough to make perfect or complete those who trusted in them (v. 1).
- The sacrifices served as a reminder of their sins (v. 3).
- Christ's sacrifice was once-for-all (v. 10) – when we appropriate His sacrifice, it is forever – we do not have to reapply it annually (v. 14).
- Because of this sacrifice, we have confidence to enter the holy place (v. 19) and are encouraged to draw near in full assurance, full knowing (v. 22).
- We are encouraged to hold fast our hope knowing that *He* is faithful (v. 23).
- Therefore, after being born-again, we need to understand there will not be any more sin offerings every year. We must live righteously knowing He perfected us once-for-all time.
- We are no longer reminded of our sins by the sacrifices of bulls and goats. We do not need to apply Christ's blood annually to cover our sins. We are cleansed once-for-all.

- The unrighteous, those who ignore the law of Moses, and those who may have a form of godliness only, will die without mercy (v. 28).
- It is important to note how the author addresses the believers in this case as "us", "we", and "you". He uses third part phraseology when discussing the others. I. e., as is the habit of some (v. 25), anyone (v. 28), he will deserve (v. 29), by which he (v. 29).
- Verse 29 discusses the severity of someone who has come in contact with the truth but disregards it. They regard as unclean the blood of the covenant. The phrase by which he was sanctified seems to indicate some knowledge of the truth.
- Verses 28 and 29 would appear by the third party language to be referring to those who forsake the assembling together (v. 25). These are likely not genuine believers as we have discussed from 1 John 2:19. So, verses 28 and 29 appear to be referring to unbelievers who actually knew the truth and then denied it. How much greater a punishment when one is being judged having had a full knowledge of the truth versus one being judged as ignorant of it.
- The Lord is the judge of His people (v. 30). Those who choose to deny the Lordship of Christ will be judged based on not being written in the Lamb's book of life. Those who are genuine believers will have their works judged for heavenly rewards.
- The author once again encourages the true believers to remember the former days (v. 32), not to throw away their confidence (v. 35) and to their need for more endurance or patience (v. 36).
- The author reminds them of the great reward of the promise of eternal life. They are to have patience keeping this promise ever before their eyes. He tells them that they are not of the class of unbelievers that shrink back to destruction. They are the ones who have a genuine faith leading to the preservation of their souls (v. 39)

Summation: _This verse is neither for nor against eternal security._

Further Explanation: This chapter contrasts the Old Covenant to the New Covenant. The passage shows the believers application of the Lord's sacrifice. It also shows the outcome of those who do not truly accept and appropriate Christ's finale atonement.

Opposing View: On the surface it seems that we cannot continue to willfully sin after being saved otherwise Christ's sacrifice no longer applies. However, the sacrifice is not referring to a losing of Christ's blood sacrifice. Rather, it is a reminder that we no longer have the sacrifice of bulls and goats to remind us that we should live holy. Now it is expected knowing Christ's sacrifice is once-for-all. Further, John makes it clear that a genuine believer cannot practice sin. The one who willfully lives a sinful lifestyle proves that the one was never genuinely converted to Christ.

Conclusion: Christ is the final sacrifice. His atonement covers our past, present and future sins without another sacrifice to atone for them.

Hebrews 12:15

> NASB: "See to it that no one comes short of the grace of God; that no root of bitterness springing up causes trouble, and by it many be defiled…"

> KJV: "Looking diligently lest any man fail of the grace of God; lest any root of bitterness springing up trouble you, and thereby many be defiled.

Context: The author just finishes encouraging the readers with stories of faith (Heb 11:1-40). He exhorts us to keep Christ as the focus of our faith (12:1-3). Then he explains why believers must go through times of discipline (12:4-11). Verses 12 through 17 are an exhortation to help others in the faith.

Comments:
- Verse 12 starts out with instructions to "strengthen" those who are weak.
- Verse 14 instructs the reader to "pursue peace" and sanctification.
- Verse 15, then, further instructs the reader to "see to" three different issues:
  - 1) That no one comes short of the grace of God
  - 2) No root of bitterness springs up and defiles many;
  - 3) That there is no immoral or godless person similar to Esau.
- It seems there are a variety of spiritual and physical conditions being addressed. The primary issue with which we are concerned is verse 15 regarding coming short of the grace of God.
- There are two phrases to be addressed:
  - "Comes short" (NASB) and "Grace of God"
- "Comes short" is the Greek word *hustereo* (Strong's #5302) meaning: "to fall short (be deficient): come behind (short), be destitute, fail, lack, suffer, need, (be in) want, be the wose[42]" and further to "fail to become a partaker[43]".
- "Grace of God" is the Greek word *charis* (Strong's #5485) which is used "pre-eminently of that kindness by which God bestows favor upon the ill-deserving, and grants to sinners the pardon of their offenses, and bids them accept of eternal salvation through Christ[44]"

Summation: *This verse is neither for nor against eternal security.*

Further Explanation: This passage is an exhortation to make sure that no one "fails to become a partaker" of the saving grace of God. By the nature of the definition of grace ("unearned and unmerited favor[45]") and by the context of the Scriptures, this passage is not referring to genuine believers "falling away" from God's unearned and unmerited favor. It is an exhortation to help people to receive the grace of God – to not "come short" of that grace, or fail to "become a partaker" of it.

Opposing View: This is to say that to "come short" means to not live up to the standard of righteousness for which a genuine believer has been called. Therefore, in the end, a believer can lose salvation if they do not live up to this standard. They will have become "defiled". However, to use this verse to support losing salvation, one has to carry the terms "come short" and "be defiled" (NASB) to drastic ends that are not supported in the context of the passages. Though we are to become more and more Christ-like in nature, a genuine believer is still a sinner saved by grace. How exactly does a genuine believer "come short" of the grace of God? At what point do we prove not worthy enough to keep our salvation – the free gift of God?

Conclusion: This verse is an exhortation to live a godly life. It does not offer a warning that not to do so will cause one to lose salvation.

Hebrews 12:25

> NASB: "See to it that you do not refuse Him who is speaking, for if those did not escape when they refused Him who warned them earth, much less shall we escape who turn away from Him who warns from heaven".

> KJV: "See that ye refuse not him that speaketh : for if they escaped not who refused him that spake on earth, much more shall we not escape, if we turn away from him that speaketh from heaven".

Context: The author is comparing the children of Israel's stubbornness and subsequent warning from God through Moses to the Jewish people receiving this letter.

Comments:
- The Greek word for "refuse" is *paraiteomai* (Strong's #3868) which is defined as "to refuse, reject[46]".
- The Greek word for "turn away from" is *apostrepho* (Strong's #654) which is defined as "to refuse, reject[47]".

- This passage is a general statement to the Jews as a people group. Even though the Hebrews letter was written to a Christian congregation substantially consisting of Jewish converts, this passage broadens the scope as the writer compares the Jewish people group as described in Exodus (the children of Israel in the wilderness). Though they know of the promise, they rejected or refused God's warnings to "repent". Those who reject Christ's warnings will also not enter into the promise – eternal salvation.
- The author warns the Jewish people as a whole in verse 25, but then assures the Jewish converts in verse 28 that "we receive a kingdom which cannot be shaken". This assurance should cause in genuine believers gratitude and acceptable service with reverence to God.

Summation: _This verse is neither for nor against eternal security._

Further Explanation: In the context of Scripture, those who turn away from Him are those who never accepted His salvation. They reject it.

Opposing View: The author states that if "we" turn away indicating that "we" refers to believers. However, "we" is referring to the Jews in general, not believers specifically. The gospel was first presented to the Jews, but they rejected it as a whole, as a people group. Then the gospel was brought to the Gentiles.

Conclusion: This passage is a warning to all those who hear about the grace of God not to reject the offer of God's grace.

James 5:19-20

> NASB: "My brethren, if any among you strays from the truth and one turns him back, let him know that he who turns a sinner from the error of his way will save his soul from death and will cover a multitude of sins".

KJV: "Brethren, if any of you do err from the truth, and one convert him; let him know that he which converteth the sinner from the error of his way shall save a soul from death, and shall hide a multitude of sins".

Context: The main theme of James is the works that follow those who believe, that is, faith without works is dead. Though he is apparently writing the letter to the Jewish Christian assembly, it becomes obvious that there are people in that assembly who are not believers as demonstrated by their works (or lack thereof).

Comments:
- Chapter 1:21 – There must be some that are not humbly receiving the saving message of the gospel of Christ (the word able to save the soul).
- Verse 22 – There must be some who are hearers only and therefore deluded.
- Verse 26 – There must be some who consider themselves religious but deceive themselves making their religion worthless.
- Chapter 2:1 – The assembly appears to welcome "visitors" or "members" differently based on their social status. No reference tells us if the statement "if a man" (NASB) refers to a believer or not.
- Verses 6, 7 – There must be some rich among them (as in verse 1) who in fact are the ones who "blaspheme the fair name by which you have been called" (verse 7).
- Verse 14 – There must be some that have faith with no works – this faith is useless (vs. 17 & 26).
- Verse 19 – Some must have the same kind of "belief" as the demons – which cannot be a saving belief.
- Verse 20 – A question posed to the foolish fellow who has an incorrect salvation theology apparently.
- Chapter 4:1 – There is conflicts and quarrels in the assembly – James addresses this statement to the general audience "you".

- Verse 2 – There are those with wicked, murderous hearts (possibly as John describes "everyone who hates his brother is a murderer; and you know that no murderer has eternal life abiding in him" – 1 John 3:15).
- Verse 4 – Are there some who are already "enemies of God"?
- Chapter 5:6 – The rich are condemning and killing the righteous man.
- So, it seems apparent that at this time, this is a mixed congregation. Although James is addressing them as "brethren", it cannot be said that every verse is about genuine believers. In fact, the Epistle of James, a Jewish convert himself, was written to a Jewish Christian assembly. James could very possibly be respectfully addressing his Jewish as well as Christian brothers. We cannot know for sure his thought on this matter. However, the audience itself is seemingly a mixed group. Otherwise, why would he be addressing all the issues that he is addressing?

Summation: *This verse is neither for nor against eternal security.*

Further Explanation: The entire epistle is written to both believers and unbelievers.

Opposing View: It would seem that this passage clearly infers that a believer can lose his or her salvation by "straying from the truth". The one straying must be the sinner referred to in verse 20 who subsequently is shown the error of his way. The good brother, then, if he is able to turn the errant brother, will be helping to save the errant brother's "soul from death". This sounds plausible on the surface. However, the author refers to "any among you" (NASB) or "Any of you" (KJV) which we discussed in the comments. The author is addressing a mixed group. We know there are some among the genuine believers that re rejecting the truth – they are "straying from it". If a brother turns one of these "straying" souls back towards the truth, the brother helps save the straying person from death.

Conclusion: This passage is an exhortation for believers to point people to Christ.

1 Peter 1:5

> NASB: "Who are protected by the power of God though faith for a salvation ready to be revealed in the last time".

> KJV: "Who are kept by the power of God through faith unto salvation ready to be revealed in the last time".

Context: Peter is writing to the believers who have been scattered, those who have been chosen and born-again.

Comments:
- Protected is the Greek word *phroueo* (Strong's #5432) meaning "to protect by guarding, to keep[48]".
- Faith is the Greek word *pistis* (Strong's #4102). This is the noun referring to the doctrine of the faith.
- Salvation is the Greek word *soteria* (Strong's #4991). In this context it is referring to the second coming of Christ – the final stage of our salvation.

Summation: This verse provides assurance for our eternal security.

Further Explanation: It is the power of God that keeps us for the salvation ready to be revealed.

Opposing View: Although it is the power of God that keeps us, He only keeps us "through faith". We must be in a state of faith in order to be kept for salvation. However, this view then says that our faith supersedes God's power. It further presumes that "through faith" means we must be in faith until the end of our natural lives. Nothing in context refers to us "believing" to the end of our natural lives.

Conclusion: This passage provides more assurance that God's power will keep us until the final resurrection in the last time.

2 Peter 1:10

> NASB: "Therefore, brethren, be all the more diligent to make certain about His calling and choosing you; for as long as you practice these things you will never stumble".

> KJV: "Wherefore the rather, brethren, give diligence to make your calling and election sure: for if ye do these things, ye shall never fall."

Context: Peter is writing to "those who have received a faith of the same kind of ours" (v. 1). He then points out the qualities of those who are growing in Christ (v. 5-7). Those with these qualities are useful and fruitful. Those without are blind and short-sighted.

Comments:
- "Make certain" is the Greek word *bebaios* (Strong's 949) meaning "that which does not fail or waver, immovable, and on which one may rely[49]". It is an adjective that means "stable, fast, firm[50]".
- Paul gives us a mirror with which to examine our hearts. As we examine the qualities in verses 5-7, we can know if we are growing in the grace or if we are blind and short-sighted. To be blind or short-sighted would be not to be looking heavenward and not to be fruitful.
- These types of believers have lost sight of the big picture. They have no eternal perspective. They "need to remember from where they have fallen; and repent and do the deeds they did at first" (Rev 2:5).
- Blind and short-sighted has also been interpreted as "spiritually blind" or in "spiritual darkness". However, this interpretation does not make sense if:

- o 1) The one who lacks these qualities has in the past been purified from his sins (v. 9);
- o 2) These are people with the same faith as Peter's (v. 1); and
- o 3) They have been established in the truth (v. 12).
- On the other hand, if short-sighted is meaning "spiritually blind" or in "darkness", then the list provides us a measuring stick to determine if indeed we are in the faith. It does not say that we were in the faith then lost salvation. We are to examine our lives and determine if we were called and chosen.

Summation: This verse is neither for nor against eternal security.

Further Explanation: Peter is encouraging believers to examine themselves and to remember that if we are growing, we will not stumble.

Opposing View: This view says that if we are doing the things listed, then we can be sure of our salvation. If we are not, then out salvation is in jeopardy. To stumble then, is to lose salvation. However, Peter is actually telling us that we should be growing in the list of qualities mentioned. If we are growing, we will not stumble. If we are not growing, we may very well stumble. We also can identify if we are truly saved by looking at the list and measuring if we are growing in the qualities of a Christian. If we are not, we should consider whether or not we are saved.

Conclusion: This passage shows us how we should be growing in character.

2 Peter 2:20-22

NASB: "For if, after they have escaped the defilements of the world by the knowledge of the Lord and Savior Jesus Christ, they are again entangled in them and overcome, the last state has become worse for them than the first. For it would be better for them not to have known the way of righteousness, than having known it, to turn away from the holy commandments handed down to them. It has happened to them according to the true proverb, 'a dog returns to its own vomit', and 'a sow, after washing, returns to wallowing in the mire'".

KJV: "For if after they have escaped the pollutions of the world through the knowledge of the Lord and Savior Jesus Christ, they are again entangled therein, and overcome, the latter end is worse with them than the beginning. For it has been better for them not to have known the way of righteousness, than, after they have known it, to turn from the holy commandment delivered unto them. But it is happened unto them according to the true proverb, the dog is turned to his own vomit again; and the sow that was washed to her wallowing in the mire".

Context: All of chapter two is exposing false teachers and false prophets.

Comments:
- "They" is a continuation from the false teachers referred to in verse 19 – the ones who are slaves of corruption. They have a form of godliness allowing them to be in the midst of the assembly. They know the way of righteousness. They had the holy commandments explained to them. They, by entering the assembly of saints, found a means of escape from the pollution of the world. Yet, as the sow, they were only externally washed and therefore returned to the mire of their inward character.

Summation: This verse is neither for nor against eternal security.

Further Explanation: It is not enough to know about Christ, He must change a person in order for the person to enjoy the benefits from Him.

Opposing View: The "last state" (latter end) must mean "hell". Therefore, those who get born-again (having escaped the pollutions of the world) and then return to their former life, will lose salvation and end up in hell. However, even if these are genuine believers, the "last state" or "latter end" is not defined in context. There is no reference to that term to mean "hell" or eternal separation from Christ. It could be said that if a genuine believer backslides like a dog returning to its vomit, that person's life will not only be miserable, but when their works are judged in the judgment of saints, they will not receive the rewards they might have received otherwise. Further, a person who is never saved, but has knowledge of the Lord and the commandments, will also live a restless life. The truth will forever be bringing condemnation in their conscience.

Conclusion: No one can rest easily once confronted with the knowledge of the Lord and Savior Jesus Christ. To know the truth is to become accountable to it.

2 Peter 3:17

> NASB: "You therefore, beloved, knowing this beforehand, be on your guard lest, being carried away by the error of unprincipled men, you fall from your own steadfastness".

> KJV: "Ye therefore, beloved, seeing ye know these things before, beware lest ye also, being led astray with the error of the wicked, fall from your own steadfastness".

Context: Peter is warning the beloved about the false teachers. He cautions the beloved that listening to these teachers may cause them to "fall" from their own steadfastness.

Comments:
- It is the "beloved", fellow Christians, genuine believers, to whom Peter is addressing this caution. He does not want them to fall.

- "Fall" is the Greek word *ekpipto* (Strong's #1601) meaning "to fall from a thing, to lose it[51]".
- "Steadfastness" is the Greek word *sterigmos* (Strong's #4740) meaning "firm condition, steadfastness: of mind[52]".

Summation: This verse is neither for nor against eternal security.

Further Explanation: Peter is concerned that the steadfastness of mind that these believers should have about the true gospel message which has been received, will not be caused to waiver by listening to false teachings.

Opposing View: Fall from your own steadfastness means to "fall from grace". In other words, lose salvation. However, to lose one's "steadfastness" cannot be interpreted as losing one's "salvation". It can be understood that these false teachings can cause a believer to waiver, maybe even backslide. Nevertheless, to carry this to an extreme that the state of wavering or backsliding either leads to a loss of salvation or is itself a condition of having lost one's salvation, would not be a proper exegesis of this passage.

Conclusion: We are cautioned to guard our minds from false teaching so as not to waiver in our resolve to serve the Lord.

1 John 2:19

> NASB: "They went out from us, but they were not really of us; for if they had been of us, they would have remained with us; but they went out, so that it would be shown that they all are not of us".

> KJV: "They went out from us, but they were not of us; for if they had been of us, they would no doubt have continued with us; but they went out, that they might be made manifest that they were not all of us".

Context: John is contrasting the believer with the unbeliever. He is warning the believers about the antichrists in their midst.

Comments:
- "They" refers to the antichrists in their midst – those who believe and teach a false gospel.
- It appears that the antichrists cannot or will not remain with the genuine believers. John says the antichrists leaving prove they were antichrists. Had they been genuine believers, they would have remained in the body.

Summation: This verse is neither for nor against eternal security.

Further Explanation: It seems that antichrists may take on an appearance of those who believe. They will blend in to the assembly for a season. However, at some point and for some reason, they left this body of believers proving they were not genuine believers.

Opposing View: This view would say that if one leaves the body of Christ, then one loses salvation. However, John never says that these were believers. In fact, he states that had they actually been genuine believers, they would have never left the faith.

Conclusion: Genuine believers and unbelievers tend to congregate together (which is evidenced even in modern church life). However, there will come a time when the wheat will be separated from the tares.

1 John 3:9

> NASB: No one who is born of God practices sin, because His seed abides in him; and he cannot sin, because he is born of God".

KJV: "Whoever is born of God doth not commit sin; for his seed remaineth in him; and he cannot sin, because he is born of God".

Context: John is describing the difference between the believer and the unbeliever.

Comments:
- The reference to sin is spoken of the present infinitive verb tense that means a continuous or repeated action. One who practices a lifestyle of sin is not one who is born of God. The one who is born of God cannot continue, because of conscience, in a lifestyle of sin. Those born of God have God's seed abiding in him.

Summation: This verse is neither for nor against eternal security.

Further Explanation: A genuine believer cannot live in a lifestyle characterized by sin. If one's lifestyle is characterized by sin, one is deceived. This is not to say a genuine believer will not commit sin – we all do. The overall character of a genuine believer's life will be of Christian growth, not of continued sinfulness.

Opposing View: n/a

Conclusion: This is another passage given to us by which we judge our conversion to be genuine or false.

1 John 5:3

NASB: These things I have written to you who believe in the name of the Son of God, so that you may know that you have eternal life.

KJV: "These things are written unto you that believe on the name of the Son of God; that ye may know that ye have eternal life, and that ye may believe on the name of the Son of God".

Context: John is writing to the believers and explaining to them who are the children of God and who are not. He is then explaining that the testimony is that God has given eternal life through His Son.

Comments:
- Those who believe can know for sure they have (not will have) eternal life.

Summation: This verse provides assurance for our eternal security.

Further Explanation: When we come to believe in Jesus, He assures us that we have at the moment attained eternal life – it is the gift of God.

Opposing View: This view says that one must be in a "continuous state of believing" to have eternal life. However, though this verb form implies such, the passage does not say that when a genuine believer discontinues believing, then the genuine believer no longer has eternal life. John did no write this passage as a warning. Rather, he wrote is as a comfort.

Conclusion: If we are genuine believers, we can rest assured that we not have the promise of eternal life.

2 John 8-9

NASB: "Watch yourselves, that you might not lose what we have accomplished, but that you may receive a full reward. Anyone who goes too far and does not abide in the teaching of Christ, does not have God; the one who abides in the teaching, he has both the Father and the Son".

KJV: "Look to yourselves, that we lose not those things which we have wrought, but that we receive a full reward. Whosoever transgresseth, and abideth not in the doctrine of Christ, hath not God. He that abideth in the doctrine of Christ, he hath both the Father and the Son".

Context: John is warning the church to watch out for false teachers – the ones who deny Jesus as coming in the flesh.

Comments:
- This appears to be a warning to the congregation at this location. Apparently, based on his comment, "what we have accomplished", John may have participated in birthing, or growing this congregation, or both.
- "Accomplished" is the Greek word *ergazomai* (Strong's #2038) meaning "to do, work out[53]". The warning is not to let the false teachers destroy the church that John and the others had labored to build.
- John desires them to receive a "full" reward. "Full" is the Greek word *pleres* (Strong's #4134) meaning "complete, lacking nothing, perfect[54]".
- "Reward" is the Greek word *misthos* (Strong's #3408) meaning "of the rewards which God bestows, or will bestow, upon good deeds and endeavors[55]"
- "Goes too far" (transgresseth: KJV) is the Greek word *parabaino* (Strong's #3845) meaning "he that transgresseth, oversteppeth, i.e., who does not hold to true doctrine[56]". This one does not hold to the truth doctrine of Christ. He is said to "not have God". The one who holds the true doctrine does have both Father and Son.
- The one "does not abide" is the one who does not have Christ. Christ has never taken abode within this one. It does not say the one who "quits" abiding.

Summation: This verse is neither for nor against eternal security.

<u>Further Explanation</u>: This shows the importance of understanding and receiving the true doctrine rather than a false doctrine.

<u>Opposing View</u>: This view believes the one who quits abiding in the true doctrine loses salvation. However, it is the one that does not obtain the true doctrine that perverts the true doctrine that does not have Christ. Verse nine points out the false teachers (the deceivers of verse seven) as those who do not have the true doctrine of Christ.

<u>Conclusion</u>: The evidence of a genuine believer is abiding in the correct doctrine of Christ. If we are not putting our trust in the true Jesus, our faith is in vain.

Jude 21

> NASB: "Keep yourselves in the love of God, waiting anxiously for the mercy of our Lord Jesus Christ to eternal life".

> KJV: "Keep yourselves in the love of God, looking for the mercy of our Lord Jesus Christ unto eternal life".

<u>Context</u>: Jude has been warning the believers of mockers that would come in the last days. He describes them as worldly-minded devoid of the Spirit (v. 19). Then he exhorts the brethren to build themselves up in the faith that is theirs as opposed to being led astray by these worldly people. He further exhorts them to pray, remain in the love of God, and wait anxiously for the fulfillment of the mercy of Christ – eternal life.

<u>Comments</u>:
- We are exhorted to "keep ourselves in the love of God" (v. 21). John describes the love of God when he says, "for this is the love of God, that we keep His commandments…" (1 John 5:3). Therefore, Jude is apparently exhorting the believers to obey the Lord, which is how we show our love for Him.

- Verse 24 shows that it is not our responsibility to "keep" ourselves in "salvation" as it is God who will "make you stand in the presence of His glory blameless with great joy" (See Jude 24 notes).

Summation: This verse is neither for nor against eternal security.

Further Explanation: The exhortation is to obey the Lord and to grow in the grace and knowledge of our Lord and Savior Jesus Christ.

Opposing View: Some might say that it is the believer's responsibility to "keep ourselves" in God's mercy and good favor so that we may "keep" eternal life. However, the "love" of God described in this passage is the "agape" love which can only be given by God to humanity. We are incapable of agape.

Conclusion: This passage is a proof text for Christian living.

Jude 24

> NASB: "Now to Him who is able to keep you from stumbling, and make you stand in the presence of His glory blameless and great with joy".

> KJV: "Now unto him that is able to keep you from falling, and to present you faultless before the presence of his glory with exceeding joy".

Context: This is the closing statement of Jude's letter. He exhorts the saints to context earnestly for the faith. He warns of false teachers, wolves in sheep's clothing, mockers. He concludes by pointing to the One who will keep the saints from falling.

Comments:
- "Keep" is the Greek word *phylasso* (Strong's #5442) which means, "to keep from being snatched away, preserve safe and unimpaired [57]".
- "Make" is the Greek word *histemi* (Strong's #2476) meaning "to cause to make or stand; to place, put, set[58]".

Summation: This verse provides assurance for our eternal security.

Further Explanation: We have security knowing Christ guards and watches over His children. Though we are responsible to grow, our eternal destiny is never in our own hands.

Opposing View: This view says that this is a promise only for those who "build themselves up in the most holy faith" (v. 20) and "keep themselves in the love of God" (v. 21). However, this is not said as an if-then statement in the book of Deuteronomy. The promise is for genuine believers – Christ will "make" us stand. Verses 20 and 21 are exhortations for Christians to grow and mature.

Conclusion: This passage provides tremendous comfort for believers.

Revelation 3:5

> NASB: "He who overcomes will thus be clothed in white garments and I will not erase his name from the book of life, and I will confess his name before My Father and before His angels".

> KJV: "He that overcometh, the same shall be clothed in white rainment; and I will not blot his name out of the book of life, but I will confess his name before my father, and before his angels".

<u>Context</u>: A warning to the church of Sardis to clean up their act, so to speak. They are doing deeds, but mostly dead works. They need to repent and get back on track.

<u>Comments</u>:
- Christ offers a rebuke and a reward. The believers at Sardis are not producing living fruit. They are told to wake up and recognize how they are living. There are a few though that had remained faithful. To them He offers the reward of walking with Him.
- "I will <u>not</u> erase" is the key phrase.
- "Not" is the Greek word *ou me* (Strong's #3364) which is a double negative meaning "never ever, not at all, by no means[59]". It is a strong denial implying an utter impossibility.

<u>Summation</u>: This verse provides assurance for our eternal security.

<u>Further Explanation</u>: This passage is a strong assurance by Christ that those whose names are in the book of life will be admitted and confessed openly. He is saying that there is no way those names will be removed.

<u>Opposing View</u>: This view says that "opposites are always true in Scripture" meaning that because Christ says He will not erase those who overcome shows that He will erase those who do not overcome. However, that is not the meaning intended based on the usage of the double negative. Further, we once again have to question what it is that must be "overcome". Finally, it is also described in Scripture that the names are written or not at the foundation of the world (see Revelation 17:8). How is it that the names of those who did not overcome (unbelievers) were written at the foundation of the world (Rev 17:8), then, erased at some later point in time? Would God not have erased those names at the foundation of the world? Alternatively, would He not have written them in the book at the foundation of the world? In God's foreknowledge, He knows the beginning to the end. He knows those who are His. He knows from the beginning those who will be His. He excluded the names of unbelievers at the beginning.

Therefore, if opposites are true, He must have included in the Book of Life all the names of believers.

Conclusion: We have great assurance that if we are genuine believers, our names will have already been written in the Lamb's Book of Life – and will remain.

Revelation 17:8

> NASB: "… and those who dwell on the earth, whose name has not been written in the book of life from the foundation of the world, will wonder when they see the beast, that he was and is not and will come".
>
> KJV: "… and they that dwell on the earth shall wonder, whose names were not written in the book of life from the foundation of the world, when they behold the beast that was, and is not, and yet is".

Context: The author is describing those who will see the beast at the apocalypse. These are the ones whose names "were not written" in the book of life from the "foundation of the world".

Comments:
- The ones "whose name has not been written in the book of life" are those who will not inherit eternal life in Christ (Rev 20:15).
- These names were not written from the "foundation of the world". Right at the beginning of time those who would not become believers were already excluded from the Lamb's Book of Life.
- Since the unbelievers were *excluded* from the book of life at the foundation of the world, it is reasonable to expect that the believers were *included* at the same time.

Summation: This verse is neither for nor against eternal security.

Further Explanation: In God's foreknowledge, He knows from the beginning who will believe and who will not.

Opposing View: n/a

Conclusion: Though we do not fully understand how God knows the beginning from the end, we trust that He does. Those that are genuine believers have had their names written in the Lamb's Book of Life from the beginning. If God knew that a believer would "lose" their salvation, He would have also excluded their names at the very beginning for this is when the unbelievers were excluded per this passage.

Revelation 17:14

> NASB: "These will wage war against the lamb, and the lamb will overcome them, because He is Lord of lords and King of kings, and those who are with Him are the called and chosen and faithful".

> KJV: "These shall make way with the Lamb, and the Lamb shall overcome them: for he is Lord of lords, and King of king: and they that are with him are called, and chosen, and faithful".

Context: There will be a war between the beast and his followers and the Lamb and His followers with the Lamb of God being the ultimate victor.

Comments:
- The ones who are with the Lamb in this battle are the "called, chosen and faithful". The question arises, are these three different groups of people or three descriptions of one group of people?
- Called is the Greek word *kletos* (Strong's #2822) which means "to call, Called, invited, welcomed, appointed. The called ones, *kletoi*, are those who have received the divine call, *klesis*

(2821), having conformed to God's saving purpose… without implying immediate obedience to the call (Mt 20:16, 22:14, cf. Rev 17:14). See *ekletos* (1588), elect[60]". Thayer's further defines it as, "invited (by God in the proclamation of the gospel) to obtain salvation in the kingdom of God through Christ[61]".

- Chosen is the Greek word *ekletos* (Strong's #1588) meaning, "chosen, elected[62]" and "to obtain salvation through Christ… hence, Christians are called… those chosen or elect of God[63]".
- Faithful is the Greek word *pistos* (Strong's #4103) meaning, "easily persuaded; believing, confiding, trusting… In the New Testament, one who trusts in God's promises… is convinced that Jesus has been raised from the dead… one who has become convinced that Jesus is the Messiah and the Author of salvation [a believer]…[64]".
- This word *pistos* as translated in this passage as faithful is the same word that in Acts 16:15 and 1 Timothy 4:10 and 6:2 is translated as "believer".

Summation: This verse is neither for nor against eternal security.

Further Explanation: It appears that the terms: called, chosen and faithful, all describe the genuine believers.

Opposing View: This view might say that the "faithful" describes those who "remained faithful to the end", those who overcome. However, the passage simply describes genuine believers. A genuine believer is faithful. This is not to say that a genuine believer will not have times of backsliding or falling into sin. No genuine believer will be perfect in this lifetime. Further, one has to read into the use of the term faithful to presuppose that it means faithful "to the end". It does not say that. In addition, the next logical question would have to be to the end of what?

Conclusion: This passage cannot be used as a proof text for losing one's salvation. It demonstrates that it is the believers who will be with the Lamb.

Revelation 22:19

> NASB: "And if anyone takes away from the words of the book of this prophesy, God will take away his part from the tree of life and from the holy city, which are written in this book".

> KJV: "And if any man shall take away from the words of the book of this prophesy, God shall take away his part out of the book of life, and out of the holy city, and from the things which are written in this book".

Context: John closes his writing with a declaration regarding those who will and those who will not have eternal life. Christ makes an invitation in the preceding verse (17), "… let the one who hears, the one who thirsts and the one who wills, come to Christ". Be alert that Christ is coming quickly.

Comments:
- The words of this passage are first spoken in Deuteronomy 4:2 and 12:32, as well as Proverbs 30:6. The statement being made is that one must obey the word of God in order to have eternal life.
- In the Old Testament, obedience was to obey the commandments by faith. In the New Testament, obedience is to God's command in Acts 17:30, "that all men everywhere should repent". One cannot add to the simplicity of the Gospel that Christ's finished work is not enough. In addition, one cannot take away from the gospel and make Christ less than He is. To do either is not to have eternal life. See notes from Revelation 17:14\ (above) regarding when the names are written in the Book of Life.

Summation: *This verse is neither for nor against eternal security.*

Further Explanation: John is identifying (as he also did so in his epistles) who are and who are not the genuine believers. Those thatadd to or take away from the truth of Scripture are not genuine believers.

Opposing View: John says God will "take away" from the Book of Life those who pervert his words. Therefore, one *can* be removed from the Book even after being entered into it. However, this contradicts Revelation 17:14 as to when unbelievers are "taken away" from the Book. Also, this verse does not say take away his "name". It says take away his "part". What exactly is that "part"?

Conclusion: John once described how to identify false prophets or false teachers – those who pervert God's word.

---

[1] Gallup, Jr., George, The Next American Spirituality, Jones Cook Communications Ministries, 2000

[2] Pentacostal Evangel, March 20, 2005

[3] IBID, Pg 18

[4] *George Barna reports of those that call themselves Christian, 40% claim to be born-again. He further clarifies this sub-group and considers seven percent of born-again Christians to be "evangelical". For all practical purposes, those Barna calls "evangelicals", we will refer to as "genuine believers" – [genuinely born-again Christians].*

[5] Kaiser Jr., William C., Davids, Peter H., Bruce, F.F., Brauch, Manfred T., Hard Sayings of the Bible, One Volume Edition, Intervarsity Press, 1996, Pg 554

[6] Thayer's Greek-English Lexicon of the New Testament, Hendrickson Publishers, Inc., Seventh Printing, March 2005, Pg. 67.

[7] Zodhiates, Spiros Lexical Aids to the New Testament as found in the Key Word Study Bible, Pgs 109, 1810 AMG Publishing, 1984, 1990 AMG International, Inc.

[8] American Heritage Dictionary, Pg 760

[9] Thayer's, Pg 336

[10] Stanley, Charles, Eternal Security: Can you be sure, Pg 186, Oliver-Nelson Books, a Division of Thomas Nelson, Inc., 1990

[11] IBID, 48

[12] Zodhiates', Pg 1814

[13] Thayer's, Pg 89

[14] Interlinear Bible: Hebrew-Greek-English, edited by Jay P. Green, Sr., Hendrickson Publishers edition, 2nd edition, 1986, Pg 796

[15] Thayer's, Pg 106

[16] 1 John 2:4

[17] Zodhiates', Pg 1856

[18] Thayer's, Pg 399

[19] Thayer's, Pg 511

[20] Zodhiates', Pg 41
[21] Zodhiates', Pg 1799
[22] Thayer's, Pg 609
[23] Zodhiates', Pg 1809
[24] Thayer's, Pg 65
[25] Zodhiates', Pg 32
[26] Thayer's, Pg 630
[27] Thayer's, Pg 63
[28] Zodhiates', Pg 25
[29] Bruce, F.F., Word Biblical Commentary, Vol 45, Pg 166
[30] Bruce, Pg 167
[31] Thayer's, Pg 102
[32] Interlinear, Pg 922
[33] Zodhiates', Pg 1879
[34] Zodhiates', Pg 70
[35] Thayer's, Pg 609
[36] Zodhiates', Pg 31
[37] Thayer's, Pg 31
[38] Zodhiates', Pg 55
[39] Zodhiates', Pg 55
[40] Thayer's, Pg 485
[41] Zodhiates', Pg 1880
[42] Zodhiates', Pg 75
[43] Thayer's, Pg 646
[44] Thayer's, Pg 666
[45] Zodhiates', Pg 1886
[46] Thayer's, Pg 482
[47] Thayer's, Pg 68
[48] http://www.biblestudytools.com/lexicons/greek/kjv/phroureo.html
[49] http://www.biblestudytools.com/lexicons/greek/nas/bebaios.html
[50] IBID
[51] Thayer's, Pg 198
[52] Thayer's, Pg 588
[53] Thayer's, Pg 247
[54] Thayer's, Pg 517
[55] Thayer's, Pg 415
[56] Thayer's, Pg 478
[57] http://www.biblestudytools.com/lexicons/greek/nas/phulasso.html
[58] http://www.biblestudytools.com/lexicons/greek/nas/histemi.html
[59] http://www.biblestudytools.com/lexicons/greek/nas/ou-me.html
[60] Zodhiates', Pg 1848

---

[61] Thayer's, Pg 350
[62] Zodhiates', Pg 1830
[63] Thayer's, Pg 197
[64] Thayer's, Pg 514

SUBJECT INDEX

[This page intentionally left blank]

SCRIPTURE INDEX

ABOUT THE AUTHOR

While serving in the United States Air Force in Sacramento, California, Kevin McCarthy made a decision on October 10, 1984 to follow Jesus Christ. He was baptized two days later in an ice-cold Jacuzzi. One month later he was asked by his pastor to take a few minutes to share his testimony publicly in what is known as the outdoor Quad at University California, Davis. Forty-five minutes later he finished his story and realized he had a passion for sharing the Gospel.

Kevin started leading evangelistic teams to malls, neighborhoods and street corners. He also took teams to San Francisco to witness on the streets and at the Wharf.

Within six months, Kevin was leading worship with his guitar and began occasionally preaching messages from the pulpit. He has lead worship and shared messages from the pulpit from time to time for thirty years.

Kevin has been married to his heaven-sent wife, Rachel, since 1986. They were engaged on their first date and married seven months later.

They have two grown children, Christopher and Noelle and a soon-to-be, Canadian son-in-law, Jaron.

Kevin has been a leader in the body of Christ for thirty years. He also speaks and facilitates workshops on the subject of leadership. His signature keynote is called Bare Naked Leadership. It is just as entertaining as it sounds.

Kevin is a veteran entrepreneur who has had numerous failures and several nice successes – one of which allowed him to become a paper millionaire for a brief moment. Paper and brief are the operative words.

As a result of making a few poor decisions, hitting bottom and having a subsequent epiphany about his worldview being riddled with horrific contradictions and a plethora of thinking errors, Kevin also speaks on the subject of personal growth and change through his two brands, Fraudcaster.org and ThinkLikeJesus.org.

For more information or to book Kevin for your event, see **www.KevinMcCarthy.com**. To comment on this book or to order more books and workbooks, visit **www.ThinkLikeJesus.Org**.

Volume Discounts

Because we understand that *Am I Really Saved?* is a great resource for any ministry and for everyone who needs to establish or reinforce a firm foundation, we want to help you make it available to everyone that you reach with the Gospel of Jesus Christ. You can purchase this book in volume at a discount so that you can make it available to everyone who needs it. You can also purchase in smaller volumes at a discount for resale in your ministry bookstores.

We offer hefty discounts for volume purchases if you give away the book to those in need. In addition, we would be happy to customize the book on large volume orders with your ministry name and/or logo. You can even add a message from your leader inside the book if you desire.

For more information on volume discounts, please contact: Inpower Books toll free at 877-527-9613.

Visit our blog at www.ThinkLikeJesus.Org.

To book Kevin McCarthy for your next service, convention, leadership meeting, retreat or Men's group, visit: www.KevinMcCarthy.com.

9 780615 964867